# Café "The Blue Danube"

## Also by Radka Yakimov

*Dreams and Shadows*
*Ashes of Wars*

# Café "The Blue Danube"

*Radka Yakimov*

# Café "The Blue Danube"

*iUniverse books may be ordered through booksellers or by contacting:*

*iUniverse*
*1663 Liberty Drive*
*Bloomington, IN 47403*
*www.iuniverse.com*
*1-800-Authors (1-800-288-4677)*

*Because of the dynamic nature of the Internet, any web addresses or links contained in this book may have changed since publication and may no longer be valid. The views expressed in this work are solely those of the author and do not necessarily reflect the views of the publisher, and the publisher hereby disclaims any responsibility for them.*

*ISBN: 978-0-5954-7672-5 (sc)*
*ISBN: 978-0-5957-1410-0 (hc)*
*ISBN: 978-0-5959-1938-3 (e)*

*Printed in the United States of America.*

*iUniverse rev. date: 12/27/2014*

# Contents

# *Preface*

## *Political correctness, multiculturalism, courtesy and all that*

Yesterday was a beautiful day in Toronto: plenty of sunshine, pleasantly warm, and no wind. It was also Gay Pride Parade Day. The previous day, only the dykes marched and drove their bikes, and the only men allowed to join were their young boys. Yesterday, though, it was everybody.

Hundreds of thousands came out to watch. The mayor, the police chief, and the fire chief all joined the parade. There were 147 floats and lots of newlyweds marching and dancing in the streets. A couple of Royal Canadian Mounties had just gotten married too and were parading in their splendid uniforms, holding hands. Some of the people in the parade said they had permanently moved to Toronto from other places (even from San Francisco), and others claimed to have traveled from across the world in order to attend the festivities.

This was not the only party going on in the city. All over the place, thousands of people were celebrating the victory of one or another country taking part in the World Cup soccer games. They were very noisy and extremely happy and patriotic. Most had wrapped themselves in one flag or another. Strangely enough, the banners and the fans did not necessarily correspond to the same ethnic group. Hmm . . .

I did not go anywhere; couldn't leave the forum—too busy defending women in general—but I saw all that on TV and was surprised to find out that one of those celebrations was going on right here, in my neighborhood, just around the corner, at an intersection of two major streets. They were the English! This was a great surprise indeed; I never knew there were so many of them around here. But, in all honesty, they might be living right under my nose and I wouldn't know that they are English. They all look the same to me by now.

It did not use to be that way in 1966. As a matter of fact, Toronto was a Protestant Scottish bastion of morality. Sundays used to be depressing: everything was closed and everybody was supposed to be in church. I do not remember if people were polite, nice, rude, or whatever, but they looked awfully stuffy. I am sure that if any of the old inhabitants were to take a look at what was going on yesterday in *their* Toronto, they would have gone back immediately to the other side.

By the way, a few days ago the results of an international survey were published here, ranking cities around the world based on how courteous their residents were. Toronto ranked third. And you wouldn't believe which one was on top: New York! Zurich was second. Go figure!

As I was typing inside and thinking about what was going outside, all I did was simply go tsk, tsk, tsk—with a smile. It was the weather, I guess.

June 26, 2006
Toronto

# PART ONE

# *Forest Hill*

Nobody who came in contact with Mrs. Margarita Karamihailov would mistake her for anything but Eastern European. It was not just her accent, but her whole appearance—the way she communicated and the attitudes she displayed under different circumstances that created this impression. She was usually well dressed, following the latest fashion with an emphasis on quality. Though, she had a particular weakness for shoes and at times, when seduced by a stylish pair, she would sacrifice comfort for looks and would spend a great deal of money without hesitation.

In her early thirties, on a trip to New York, she had an experience that was somewhat confusing, but had led her to believe for a while that she blended well in the North American milieu. It happened in the hotel where she, her husband, and their young daughter were staying during a short vacation. Just back from a sightseeing tour, on her way up to their room, she entered the elevator, holding her daughter in her arms. An elderly, fragile-looking woman followed them in before the door slammed closed. Jessica, Mrs. Karamihailov's daughter, was a two-years-old, pretty, blond little thing with huge eyes, long, dark eyelashes and a cute button nose. The white-haired, pleasant-looking lady seemed taken by the little girl. She smiled warmly at the child.

"Hello. What is your name?" the woman asked Jessica in a most friendly way.

Pressing against her mother, Jessica kept a stubborn silence. Margarita felt obliged to answer the polite old woman.

"Jessica," she said, readjusting her arms around the little girl.

"Oh, what a nice name, indeed," remarked the old lady. Shifting her gaze from the child to the mother, she continued.

"Where are you from?"

Before Mrs. Karamihailov could answer, the woman added, "Are you from Boston?"

"No . . ."

Again she was prevented from completing the sentence; the elevator had suddenly come to a stop and the old lady had to exit in a hurry. Charmingly polite right up to the last moment, she disappeared with a wave of her hand and a cheerful, "Bye."

For the rest of the ride up to their floor, Margarita remained alone with her daughter, flushed with excitement. She was surprised and pleased to be mistaken for a North American, for she was still craving acceptance.

Years have passed since then. She has grown older and, as she thought, wiser, for she had outgrown her uncertainties about where she belonged or how she was perceived. Now, it took a lot to upset her or please her on that account.

Physically she had changed as well. Her figure had filled out and the features of her face had grown heavier. The resemblance to her mother was becoming ever so close.

Meanwhile, life was good for the Karamihailov family. Mr. Karamihailov was a successful businessman and Mrs. Karamihailov had an equally successful practice as a dentist. Their two daughters—the family had increased by one more girl—received the best possible education, attending private schools and reputable universities. Home was a comfortable executive townhouse in close proximity to the prestigious district of Forest Hill. Both husband and wife drove high-performance German cars and led privileged lifestyles. This included the weekly services of a cleaning lady and a gardener to take care of the maintenance of the small but professionally landscaped backyard. During the winter months, the driveway, as well as the paths around the house, was kept clean of snow by a hired snow removal service.

Their present residence was not their first home. As a matter of fact, they had owned a couple of different houses before this one. They had sold both at a profit, which allowed them to improve their housing situation each time they moved.

Strangely, each one was bought on an impulse. House hunting—going to open houses—was their hobby. Salesmen seemed to sense their propensity to make big decisions on the spur of the moment, but never succeeded in drawing them into actions they would later regret. So the fun was never spoiled.

However, the circumstances of their life had changed. Jessica, the older of their two daughters, had married, and Andrea, their youngest, had moved out of the family abode. For now, the Karamihailovs had no plans of changing their address. Still, the habits of going to open houses, of following the trends in the construction industry, and of keeping up with the fluctuation in prices remained. Furthermore, they had earned somewhat of a reputation among their friends as experts in the real estate business, and at least for vanity's sake, they felt compelled to keep informed.

It was a cool autumn day. It had been raining earlier. Also, it was Sunday and Margarita felt a touch of cabin fever. She had spent the morning doing some paperwork and felt drained. She thought that a walk around the neighborhood would refresh her.

Absent-mindedly, she took out a car coat and a pair of old shoes from a closet in the entrance hall. The coat was an old, out-of-fashion tweed jacket, with slightly worn lining that hung below the hem of the garment—something that had escaped her attention. Its charcoal shade clashed with the tint of her heavy brown skirt, which in turn was mismatched with the rest of her outfit. The out-of-shape black shoes had long ago lost their luster. In short, Mrs. Karamihailov looked far from her best, even though she made a last-minute attempt to improve her appearance.

As she opened the door, ready to step out, she got a glimpse of her pasty face and tousled hair in the mirror on the wall of the entrance hall, opposite the closet. Startled, she closed the door, pulled some lipstick from her pocket, and applied a thick layer of deep red color on her lips. Then she smoothed her hair with the palms of her hands and, without any further delay, left the house.

Margarita felt the cool air brush against her face and took a deep breath, inhaling the refreshing scents of cut grass and rain-washed junipers. After a brief hesitation, considering which direction to take, she turned left, intent on going west toward Forest Hill, an enclave of prestigious, large homes and quiet streets lined by mature trees and beautifully landscaped yards. All of these exclusive, well-built and meticulously maintained estates were also some of the most expensive in the city.

It was a pleasant and peaceful place for walkers and joggers. Strangers greeted each other politely and always moved out of the way for joggers and baby carriages in a display of civilized manners and a friendly community spirit.

For more than an hour, Margarita leisurely meandered through the streets, her hands tucked into her pockets. Occasionally, she would pause to enjoy the beauty of the shrubs covered in fragrant blossoms, to look at a spectacular arrangement of potted flowers, or to contemplate the façade of a recently renovated mansion. The exercise had refreshed her, but was beginning to challenge her endurance. It was time to head back home.

She had just made a final turn into the way leading to her street when she almost ran over an open house sign. A short distance farther to her right stood a brand new house with a French façade. In its front yard was another sign pointing toward its entrance, welcoming everybody to inspect the premises. A black Mercedes parked by the curb was the only car to be seen.

Giving in to the old familiar urge to go and have a look, Margarita turned the corner and walked toward the house.

The terrain around the dwelling looked like a construction site. A row of concrete slabs laid across the front yard, resting over the loose earth, constituted a temporary path that led to the front entrance: a handsome door made of wrought iron and glass, an elegant combination of materials of strength and lightness. The intricate design of the metal allowed an ample view of the spacious interior of the house, enough to arouse one's curiosity.

Margarita walked down the path and gave the closed door a firm push. It did not budge. Undeterred, she tried again, but to no avail. She noticed the doorbell mounted to the right of the doorframe, and considering the possibility that the door might be locked, she pressed the button. There was no movement inside as far as she could determine. Still, Margarita went on ringing until finally the door opened.

Sort of.

A well-groomed man in his early forties appeared at the doorway. His left shoulder rested against the doorframe, his right hand was placed on the door handle, and his body obstructed the narrow opening. His eyes looked down sternly at Mrs. Karamihailov standing a step below the threshold of the house.

"Yes?" he inquired curtly.

For a moment Margarita just stood there, nonplussed.

"You are holding an open house, aren't you?" she asked. "I saw the sign. I'd like to see the house."

She started lurching forward, ready to step up and go inside. The man pulled the handle even tighter, inching toward her, determined to keep her out.

Margarita was puzzled.

"Aren't you Mr. Cunningham, the sales representative?" She asked bewildered, "Your name is on the sign."

"Yes, I am Mr. Cunningham," the man said with the same curt blend of impatience and annoyance.

"Then, Mr. Cunningham, will you let me in? I would like to see the house."

"I can't let you in. You have no appointment."

"There is no mention on the sign that an appointment is necessary."

"The price range of the house is such that we require a bank statement before we show the premises to anybody," he said. "Can you show me a bank statement?"

Mrs. Karamihailov's face acquired an ash color; her breathing became shallow and laborious. Meanwhile, Mr. Cunningham's face had turned red and his eyes flashed provocatively.

With a great effort Mrs. Karamihailov tried to collect herself, and level one last blow at the salesman—filled with as much contempt and indignation as she could muster.

"Mr. Cunningham, I live close by and own a house just like this one," she said. "How *dare* you treat me this way?"

"Well, then, you would have no problem providing a bank statement, would you?" he shot back in a voice full of sarcasm, slamming the door in her face.

There was nothing Mrs. Karamihailov could do but turn around and walk away from the attractive house with white stone-covered façade and French windows protected halfway by decorative wrought iron railings. In the heat of her frustration and humiliation, she had compared it to her smaller and less-pretentious home. The realization of that had deepened her sense of embarrassment and resentment. The emotional state she had fallen into was now affecting her physically.

About a block away from the house, she had to stop, unable to continue walking, afraid her legs would not obey her any farther. She plunged her hand into her pocket, searching for a small pillbox. Relieved to find it, she opened it, took out a small, pale-blue tablet, and broke it in half. Then she popped one of the pieces in her mouth and returned the other half to the pillbox.

By the time she reached her house, her heart had resumed its normal rhythm and her head felt a little giddy. The first thing she did in her home was change from the clothes she was wearing into her favorite housecoat, and then stretched herself on her comfortable couch in front of the television set.

A couple of hours later, Mr. Karamihailov came home to find his wife stone-faced, staring at the television. He was not alone. Their older daughter, Jessica, and her husband, Jim, were accompanying him. The three of them seemed quite excited; Jessica was positively beaming.

"Mom, get dressed," she said. "We have to show you something!"

In their state of exuberance, none of the three noticed Mrs. Karamihailov's mood. As a matter of fact, it was doubtful that Mrs. Karamihailov would have discussed her feelings even if anybody had noticed the state she was in.

She got up and changed back into the same clothes she had taken off earlier and dumped in a pile on the nearby armchair. After slipping her feet into the same old shoes, she followed her husband to the car parked in the driveway. Silently, she squeezed herself in the backseat. Seated in the front, Jessica kept on talking.

"It will be a short drive, mom," she said. "We could have walked there, but we are pressed for time."

Abruptly she paused.

"You will see," Jessica added. "It is a surprise!"

A short time later, the car came to a stop. Mrs. Karamihailov, who was sharing the backseat with her husband, had not said a word. She seemed preoccupied and completely disinterested in her surroundings. At the end of the short trip, she had no idea where she was, or what was the reason for all the excitement.

As she stepped out of the car and onto the sidewalk and raised her eyes, she fell into a state of total disbelief. She was standing in front of the very same handsome house with the French façade where only a short couple of hours earlier, she had suffered one of the worst experiences she could remember, and one she wanted desperately to forget.

Jessica, Jim, and Mr. Karamihailov were already inside when she reached the wide-open doorway. Mr. Cunningham was standing by, addressing them with most obliging attention. On her way toward the front door, Mrs. Karamihailov had a hard time walking straight. A couple of times she had lost her footing, and she ended up stepping in the wet dirt beside the concrete slabs covering the pathway. Some mud had stuck to the soles of her shoes, and some of the moisture had penetrated the shoe leather.

When Mr. Cunningham noticed her, in a matter of seconds, he went through several stages of reaction, ending finally in a state similar to hers. His first thought was, "The gall of that woman!" But a moment later, a preposterous idea crossed his mind: "Is it possible?" That is when he was overcome by a sense of deep disbelief.

The awkward meeting between Mrs. Karamihailov and Mr. Cunningham passed unnoticed by the rest. As soon as Mrs. Karamihailov entered the vast hallway, Jessica introduced her to Mr. Cunningham,

"This is my mother, Dr. Karamihailov," she said. "Thank you for waiting and giving us time to bring her to see the place." Putting her arm around her mother's shoulders, she continued, "Without her approval, we wouldn't even consider making the offer."

Turning back to her mother, Jessica went further.

"Mom, on our way back from the office we drove by and saw the house. We liked it so much!" She said, laughing with delight.

Jessica and Jim had been talking about getting a newer, bigger house since they were considering starting a family. Financially, they were doing very well indeed.

Earlier that morning, they had gone to the office, accompanied by Mr. Karamihailov, to work on an urgent project. Mr. Karamihailov had recently split his business and created a new company, which was now run by his older daughter and his son-in-law. It had been a very successful business move.

However, it had never crossed Mrs. Karamihailov's mind that Jessica and her husband were looking for a house in earnest. And it had positively not dawned on her a few hours earlier.

While considering all this, Margarita could hear her daughter going on.

"It is close by your place," Jessica said. "We can even have a car pool with Dad. Dad also likes it! Now, it is up to you!"

After a short pause, giving some time to her mother to contemplate all she had just said, Jessica concluded, "Mom, come on. Let me show you the house. Is it all right with you, Mr. Cunningham?"

Meanwhile, Mr. Cunningham had moved farther back from the group and was standing by the door in a stiff posture with a slightly frazzled expression across his face. A sign attached to the inside of the doorframe read, "Please remove your shoes." Following the instructions, Jessica, Jim, and Mr. Karamihailov were walking across the foyer shoeless, their feet clad in socks. On the other hand, Mrs. Karamihailov had kept her shoes on, leaving unseemly muddy footprints over the spotless white marble floor.

"Mom, read the sign. Mom!" Jessica blurted, pointing to the sign.

"Oh!" Mrs. Karamihailov said, obviously unperturbed, "You know how much I hate to take off my shoes. I am sure Mr. Cunningham wouldn't mind."

Mr. Cunningham shrugged slightly, indicating that he did not mind indeed. While the four visitors went on a tour of the premises, he remained on the main floor, rooted to the same spot, holding his hands folded behind his back.

The roomy house was furnished sparsely but elegantly, thus allowing people with differing tastes to feel comfortable, giving them just a hint of the possibilities offered by all that space. Also, it did not distract the attention of the discriminating and knowledgeable customer from the subtle finishing touches and the excellence of the workmanship. It was a beautiful house, and Mrs. Karamihailov said so as she emerged from the last of the bathrooms on the second floor, far away from earshot of Mr. Cunningham.

Half an hour later, they were ready to leave.

"We will be in touch with our lawyer and will make an offer as soon as possible, as discussed before," Jessica said. "By the way, my mother likes the house."

Mr. Cunningham shook Jessica's hand and remarked, "I am glad, Mrs. Ballantyne, that your mother liked the house; she has excellent taste."

Mrs. Karamihailov just smiled. However, on her way toward the exit, not addressing anybody in particular, but loud enough to be heard by anybody standing close by, she commented in an acid voice. "Nice house, indeed. Not as large as ours, but good enough—at least for awhile."

Mr. Cunningham stepped respectfully aside letting her pass through the wide-open doorway.

# Café "The Blue Danube"

A well-set man with a surly face and unkempt hair sat at a small round table, all alone, outside the café. His briefcase rested on a chair next to him. In front of him there was a small cup of espresso coffee, which he had barely touched. His stiff posture and constantly shifting gaze along the street exuded impatience and anticipation.

It was early morning. The café, as well as the patio in front of it, was empty. Large, folded sun umbrellas were lined up along the low, decorative, wrought-iron fence. Arranged between them, dark-green junipers potted in large clay pots further separated the patio from the sidewalk. The interior of the café, seen from the street through the wide-open door, appeared like a deep, cavernous hole. On the right side of the entrance, close to the front, the outlines of a bar were discernible. The rest was hidden in darkness.

Inside, seated at a table close to the window, was the proprietor, a heavy-set mustached man reading a newspaper while occasionally sipping black coffee from a large mug.

A younger man in his twenties appeared from a side street. He entered the patio, quickly navigating his way between the tables until he reached the one occupied by the man. He pulled up an empty chair and installed himself in front of him. Immediately he started talking.

"Hi," he said. "Sorry I'm late. Had to work late last night."

"Never mind," the older man said, stretching his arm and picking up the brown envelope the young man had laid on the table. "How did it go?"

"Fine," answered the younger man with a shrug of the shoulders. He did not sound very convincing.

The older man was going through a pile of papers he had pulled from inside the envelope, examining them with professional expedience, when the younger man broke the silence with a hint of anxiety in his voice.

"What exactly is a conditional order of departure?" he asked.

"Didn't you ask them to explain it to you?" And after a pause, the older man added confidently, "Don't worry, it won't come to that," his voice modulating soothingly.

"Yes, I did," the younger man said. "But I wanted to hear it from you."

The conversation was in a foreign language; it sounded hard and hissing—Eastern European, most probably Slavic.

Finally, the older man stopped shuffling the papers and put them back in the envelope, which he deposited in his briefcase.

"Well, everything's here," he said. "I'll take care of the forms. When I am ready, I'll give you a call. You'll have to sign and send them before the due date."

The older man sounded relaxed and confident.

"There'll be no problem," he continued. "I'll contact the lawyer and we'll get together to discuss the story. Did you have your medical examination?"

"No, not yet. They gave me a list of names of doctors to select from. It is with the rest of the papers."

"I saw it. No need for the list. I'll give you the name and address of a doctor who speaks the language. No problem."

The older man produced a cellular phone from one of his pockets, and threw an apologetic half-smile into the younger man's direction.

"Hello Maria. How are things? Is the client there? Ugh, I am sorry, got delayed with another job. I'm coming right away. Thanks!"

The conversation was in English. The man got up hastily from his chair, lifted the cup of already-cold coffee to his lips, and emptied it in one gulp.

Then, switching back to the foreign language, he said. "I'm off. Have an appointment with immigration."

Before he disappeared from the young man's sight, who was still sitting quietly at the table in a state of docile attention, the older man shot one last comment at him: "The hearing's in three months. Not much time left. I'll give you a call," and without waiting for a reply, he brusquely walked away.

The owner of Café "The Blue Danube" was born and raised in a town located on the banks of the renowned river. He had left his birthplace less than a dozen years earlier in search of a new life. Thousands of kilometers away, he found his luck. But like most immigrants, part of his heart remained in his native land.

He decided to name his café after the river that dominated his memories, not only for sentimental reasons but also out of determination to proclaim his European identity. While many knew of the river, very few knew much about his country.

The café became a meeting-place for his compatriots. The *old* immigrants came mainly for the food and the entertainment: a couple of times a week, there were live performances provided by musicians and singers, some imported from the old country. The *new* immigrants came, compelled by the need to meet people like themselves, to make contacts, to relax in a familiar environment, and to hear their native tongue, as well as to enjoy their favorite food.

It was also a place where people met on business.

The flood of immigrants from Eastern Europe had created a need for a new category of paralegals who specialized in the intricacies of the immigration policy and helped the bewildered new refugees get what they wanted: landed immigrant status. It was this kind of business that had brought the two men together this particular morning. The younger man had his first interview the day before, and had cleared the first hurdle: his refugee claim was accepted. But it would take a long time for the process to be completed.

The temperature had climbed and the humidity had increased; the sun had changed its position in the sky. Its rays, filtering through the now-open umbrellas threw soft shadows over the patio and part of the sidewalk. The bright light bathing the windows dispelled the dusk inside the café.

It was midday. Workers from the nearby offices, descending upon the restaurants and shops along the street, were drifting into the patio of Café "The Blue Danube". The liveliness and bustle were accentuated by a number of waiters busily navigating their way between the crowded tables, scurrying back and forth to and from the kitchen, carrying trays covered with salad bowls, mineral water, beer, and coffee.

Inside, the deep and narrow interior of the café was pleasantly cool. A couple of men advanced in age sat at a table far to the back. Their clothes reflected tastes of past decades. One was a distinguished looking man who, even accounting for the normal shrinkage of age, still cut an impressive figure. The other man was shorter, thin, and fragile, yet, still youthful in appearance—an impression probably created by the mop of white hair covering his head. Each man had a large cup of coffee set in front of him. The deferential and friendly manner in which the proprietor kept on stopping by their table just to exchange a word or two, suggested they were regulars and were well respected by the owner.

The two were involved in a conversation inspired by an event that had taken place a few days earlier: a seminar with guest speakers from the old country. The well-organized and widely promoted event had attracted a large audience. The auditorium had been filled to capacity and both men had attended. During the period that followed the speeches, a number of questions had been raised, some provocative, dealing with old, unresolved issues. Obviously agitated, the smaller man was making a point:

"How many people died fighting in the name of unification? My father was wounded during the war in 1918. We can't forget the sacrifices these generations made. And now, what kind of politicians are these? Betraying sacred causes!" His eyes were flashing angrily; his hands were gesticulating widely.

In contrast to the passion displayed by his friend, the taller man maintained a dignified silence, composed and aloof, exuding the superiority of a person secure in his righteousness. His positions were clear and he had no desire to elaborate them again.

The men had known each other for more than fifty years. Both had come here at the end of the Second World War, on the heels of the adverse changes the conflict had brought to their native land. The smaller man had come via the refugee camps and the taller man had arrived straight from a Western European university—one year shy of graduating as a mechanical engineer. Now, the generation of that post-war wave of immigrants was growing older and shrinking.

Politics had always played a predominant role in their lives. They had passionately argued about every issue that had crept onto the world-stage during their lifetime and was relevant to their central concern—the state of affairs in their native country—staunchly defended their allegiances to parties and causes that belonged to their past. And while their native country had moved in a new direction, they had stubbornly stuck to the old course. The new generation deemed them irrelevant.

This new, changed world presented them also with new challenges—on a strictly personal level—ones they had never contemplated, and thus, felt completely unprepared to deal with. Finally, after half a century spent in exile, they could go back home. To some of those who did, it brought disillusionment and hurt; hardly anybody was interested in their travails. The place they encountered only superficially resembled the place they had carried in their memories and hearts for so long. Others realized for the first time how estranged from the old country they had become and how deep their roots had grown into the new one. But branded forever as immigrants by the accents they could never overcome, they were to remain forever stuck between the two worlds.

The conversation gradually drifted in another direction—into a new, growing issue within their church. The church was not just a place for worship; it was the focus of existence for the old immigrants, the center of their social activities, the promulgator of old traditions extending the connection of the old country to the future generations.

"The priest has to go," the smaller man said. "He refuses to learn English. We are losing the young people."

He was adamant; each statement was made in a categorical voice and emphasized by a categorical gesture.

"The new immigrants think otherwise," said the taller man.

"Bah, the new immigrants," the smaller man echoed the words contemptuously. "They are not church-going people. Shame on them! Don't know how to dress for church; don't know how to make the sign of the cross. What can you expect from people brought up like heathens?"

"Many are well-educated professionals," the tall man added, placating the other man in an effort to maintain a dialogue and keep the conversation from deteriorating into a show of unrestrained emotional outbursts.

A bit later, though, he ruefully continued.

"At church last Sunday, I hardly recognized anybody. None of the old crowd, instead, all new, unfamiliar faces."

"Exactly! This is why I am not going to church anymore!" pointed out the shorter man stubbornly.

The discussion came to an abrupt end, interrupted with the entrance into the café of a well-groomed older woman carrying a shopping bag. The face of the shorter man lightened up. The café's proprietor also seemed pleased to see her. He approached the table, politely pulled out a chair for her, and took her order.

As she settled in comfortably with her bag on her knees and a large cup of coffee in front of her, she shoved her arm into the bag and pulled out a colorful package of an educational toy designated for a young child from five to eight years of age.

"Finally found it. I am so glad," she said, turning towards the tall man, her eyes beaming with joy. "It is Amy's birthday in a couple of days."

Half an hour later, the short man and the woman—his wife—were gone. A somewhat younger, fair man had joined the tall man at the table. After exchanging greetings with his friend, as well as with the proprietor, he pointed to the pile of folded newspapers he had placed in front of the older man.

"Those are some newspapers from the old country," he said. "You can have them."

Meanwhile, the waiter had served him, and for a while, he fell quiet, busily preparing his coffee the way he liked it: very sweet, and with plenty of milk. Then he added, with a measure of irritation in his voice, "The same old stories. The same mentality, the same crooks blaming 'the changes' for the whole mess. What changes are they talking about? Basically, nothing has changed!"

The tall man pulled the stack of newspapers toward him and glanced at the headlines on the front page of the paper on top of the pile. He spent a few moments leafing through the pages absentmindedly.

"I am still contemplating one last visit to the old country before I get too old to travel," he remarked in a pensive voice. "It is different with you. You are younger, and you have relatives and friends over there. But what am I going for? There is hardly anybody left there to go to."

After a moment's pause, with a note of nostalgia in his voice, he concluded,

"Still, it will be nice to go back once more, probably for the last time . . ."

The morning had now evolved into a warm and sunny afternoon, perfect for sitting outside, eating frozen yogurt or ice cream, and watching the people go by. There were a couple of hours left till the end of the working day and the patio was almost empty. The dark green leaves of the potted sweet geraniums under the windows were drooping sadly, all their freshness sucked up by the hot sun. Only a few tables were occupied.

A stocky middle-aged man wearing a black leather jacket, despite the heat, halted in front of the café, scrutinizing the place from the sidewalk. Meanwhile, the much younger man accompanying him continued walking inside without any hesitation. Slowly crossing the patio while glancing around, he reached the open door and peeked inside. Completing his task, he immediately went back to fetch his stocky companion and ushered him to a table near the window, where a man in his early sixties was sitting alone. At the sight of the two men coming through the open door, he jumped from his seat and stretched out his arm for a handshake.

"Stephen! Greetings," he said. "What a surprise!"

The two older men embraced.

"Peter! Finally, we meet again! Hard to believe it!"

A few steps away, the younger man stood by, watching. Before sitting down, Stephen turned to him.

"This is Tommy, my guide," he told Peter. "He's been living here for a couple of years."

Indeed, it had been a long time since the cousins had seen each other. Peter had left in the sixties when Stephen was just a toddler. In the subsequent span of more than thirty-five years, they had known each other only from a few photographs—fading images of fleeting moments from places on the opposite ends of the vast distance that separated them.

Their relationship was close—they shared a common grandmother. However, being the offspring of different grandfathers, they did not share a common family name. That was fortunate for his uncles and their families, for, after Peter ran away, they could easily disassociate themselves from him.

For his part, Peter had no desire to maintain contact with anybody he had left behind, that is to say, except for his parents. He married a Canadian, settled in the suburbs, and put his past life behind him. His mother died without seeing him again, or meeting his wife and children. That had hardened him even further.

Back home, Peter's relatives had little to complain about. Stephen's father, Todor, had a comfortable position within the ministry of agriculture—he had married a woman who came from the right background. His brother, Boris, was faring even better. In order to protect their careers after Peter's defection to the West, all connection with his uncles, aunts, and cousins had to cease.

Estrangement followed. It was bridged only on one occasion: when his Uncle Boris helped Peter's father acquire an external passport and exit visa allowing him to visit his son abroad. It was not a small matter, and Peter was very grateful. However, after his father's passing, he again lost track of his relatives.

Ten years had gone by since the changes in his native country had occurred. But a deep-seated bitterness about the past kept Peter from going back.

Meanwhile, his cousins had lost a lot, but not all. Actually, in some way, they were better off now than before as they had the advantage of being raised with confidence and expectations of a secure future. They may have lost the expectations, but they were still confident people and without many scruples to hold them back. Also, new opportunities, far greater than they could ever have imagined within the confines of their small home country, were coming their way. The world had become whole again, and, ironically, they had become the budding businessmen looking forward to a future of unlimited possibilities.

The time had come to establish connections with their Western cousin.

"Here's something for you from the old country," said Stephen while handing Peter a small bag. "An heirloom—a tablecloth embroidered by our grandmother. My wife kept it for you throughout the years."

Peter took out the folded cloth and squeezed it slightly between the palms of his hands, but before opening it, he changed his mind and put it back, pushing the bag away to the far end of the table.

"Thanks," he said simply, assuming a more pensive attitude.

It seemed that his enthusiasm had dissipated since the initial outburst of excitement, and now he fell into silence.

The unexpected phone call from Stephen earlier that morning had surprised him greatly. His cousin had told him that he was just passing through the city on his way to a place south of the border where he had some business. He expressed a desire to meet in the afternoon, sometime during the few spare hours he had to waste in the city. A friend of his son Ivo frequented a café in a convenient downtown location and was free and willing to take him there. Stephen had also told Peter that Ivo was planning to leave the old country and possibly come here. Wouldn't it be nice to have a relative to help him get settled? All was said in jest.

A decade earlier, Peter and his wife had moved north, away from the big city, to a small picturesque town. The city was growing too fast; it was hard to keep up with the changes, and not everyone liked what it was turning into.

Peter did not know the café, so he left early to give himself plenty of time to locate it. As it happened, he found the café easily, and arrived much earlier than he had anticipated. While waiting for his cousin, he had grown anxious and excited. But now, seated across from him, he was at a loss for words.

"Tell me something about your family, about your wife, children," Stephen said. "I understand that you have retired? How is life for a pensioner here?"

Without giving Peter a chance to answer, Stephen continued.

"There is no life for pensioners in the old country. Things are bad—really bad. No jobs for the young and as far as the old people . . . a pitiful existence. Can't pay the heating and electricity bills."

Peter was taken aback. Weary of any talk that could disturb his emotional equilibrium, he was determined to keep the conversation within the limits he had set for himself. He had made up his mind long ago not to discuss politics with his compatriots. With time, his outlook on life had changed, and therefore he saw the world through a different prism than most of them did. It was useless to discuss matters that always ended in arguments.

It was time to change the subject.

"How is Uncle Boris?" Peter asked.

"Uncle Boris?" Stephen was caught by surprise." Didn't you know? He died last year. Didn't anybody write you?"

Peter was getting annoyed.

"Write? Who would write me?" he snapped back, thinking, *What is he talking about? When did anyone write to me ever?*

"Oh, well," Stephen said. "It was a sad affair. He died from grief."

Peter was shocked.

"What do you mean? What happened?"

It was hard for Peter to believe that his uncle had tragically succumbed to a feeling. He was one tough man.

Stephen took some time before answering.

"Do you remember his apartment?" he asked. "Had to move out. Got affected by the restitution. The former owners took it back. He sued, fought hard for a couple of years, but in the end, lost. Had to move to the suburbs, to an apartment he got in exchange. Imagine, thrown out of his home; imagine the effect on his children who had grown up there!"

In a voice laden with sympathy, he continued:

"He simply couldn't take it. Died from grief."

Peter remembered his uncle's spacious, comfortable apartment, located in one of the most desirable districts of the city. But he also remembered how his uncle took possession of it after the owners were exiled and their properties were confiscated.

"The old owner must have died," Peter said. "Who got the apartment?"

"His sons got it." Stephen's answer was terse and resentful.

*So, where's the injustice?* thought Peter.

Suddenly, he was overcome by discomfort. It was time to change the subject again.

"How is Aunt Ivanka doing?" he asked.

Following the introductions upon arriving at the café, Tommy—the young fellow who was accompanying Stephen—had excused himself, leaving the two cousins to talk in private. On his way in, he had spotted an acquaintance sitting alone at a table on the patio, enjoying a drink. After a moment of hesitation, considering the options of how to spend the waiting time, he decided to join her.

Settled by the low fence, sipping beer and smoking cigarettes, they watched the people pass by on the sidewalk and the steady flow of cars along the road, occasionally exchanging comments about this and that. Both had other things on their minds, and it was convenience rather than interest that had brought Tommy to her table. The conversation of the older men did not concern him at all. As a matter of fact, it bored him. What they were probably talking about was irrelevant, old-time stuff, and as far as he was concerned, it should be forgotten. He had come to this country with one set goal to achieve: to make money, one way or another. It was clear that things were not going to get better anytime soon in the old country, and he had no patience to wait for that to happen.

Tommy's friend shared his doubts, and she was just as determined and impatient to get the best out of life as soon as possible.

The traffic situation in the city had worsened in the last decade; the rush hours kept growing longer and starting earlier. The highways were crowded with cars and big trucks moving in both directions from early morning until late evening, day in and day out.

The thought of the trip back home was beginning to worry Peter. Stephen also had to rush; there were just a few hours left till his scheduled flight to New York later that evening. Emptying his cup of coffee in haste, Peter rose. His cousin followed, leaving a couple of empty beer bottles on the table. Awkwardly, Peter reached in his pocket and pulled out an envelope.

"Something for Aunt Ivanka," he said, handing it to Stephen.

Aunt Ivanka was Stephen's mother. It was on impulse that he had brought a small sum of money, just in case his cousin confronted him with a request from a relative in need. Nothing of that sort happened, but he was told that Uncle Todor—Stephen's father—had passed away recently. That meant increased financial hardship for Aunt Ivanka. Peter was pleased with himself for coming prepared—the envelope came in very handy, indeed.

The cousins proceeded toward the patio, the bag containing the family heirloom in Peter's hand. As soon as he saw them, Tommy's face brightened—an indication of obvious relief; he jumped to his feet, waved to his acquaintance, and with just a "Ciao," joined the two older men.

"Well, it was nice to see you," Peter said "Regards to all back home, and next time you visit the city, come to my house and spend some time with my family. Get to know my wife, children, grandchildren . . ."

"Thanks for the invitation," Stephen said. "We'll do it. Too bad I couldn't manage it now, but you can see, this is a business trip. I am trying—I am hoping—to start something, and if things work out . . ."

He did not have to finish the sentence—the implications were clear. After an embrace and a couple of mutual pats on the shoulders, the two cousins separated, and each went on his way.

As the three men were leaving, a man in a hurry brushed against them on his way into the café.

"Sorry to keep you waiting," the man said, plopping down into the seat Tommy had vacated just a moment earlier.

"It is all right," the young woman replied while squashing the cigarette butt against the inside of an empty beer glass.

The man gazed at her with unabashed ardor. His smiling blue eyes were fixed on her striking, somewhat exotic face with its dark brown, wide-set eyes and her black hair pulled back and tied in a knot behind the nape of her head.

"Let's go," she snapped as she got up and grabbed him by the hand.

She had something on her mind that could not wait. Spotting the picture of an attractive woman displayed on a small poster attached to the inside of the windowpane, the man's blue eyes lit again with an appreciative glee. Below the portrait in bold letters was written:

*"TANYA MIHAILOVA"*
*One performance only-Aug. 11.*
*Starting at 8 o'clock.*

◆          ◆          ◆

The patio outside the café was almost abandoned while the inside was packed, filled to capacity. All the tables were occupied and a few extra ones were squeezed together to accommodate the large crowd. The air was thick with cigarette smoke and permeated by the piquant aroma of grilled meat and the sharp scent of pickled or marinated vegetables.

In the far corner of the room, behind the tables occupied by adults, a score of restless teens dallied around, conversing loudly in English. The peculiar sounds of a foreign language seemed to compete with the clatter of utensils for the attention of the mostly young and middle-aged public.

Midway along the wall opposite the bar was a platform. On the floor below and beside it was a square table covered with an embroidered tablecloth. A pile of compact disks and tapes were stacked to one side of it and next to them, a stack of posters—the same as the one displayed in the window—were strewn about, available to anyone. This was where Tanya Mihailova would be going to sign autographs at the end of her performance.

Meanwhile, the patrons were busily emptying plates of food and glasses of wine, beer, and what not. Waiters carrying trays covered with dishes and bottles had a hard time clearing the tables to make room for the new orders.

Most had finished with their main courses and were digging into their favorite dessert, baklava, when Tanya Mihailova stepped on to the platform to loud applause. All conversations ceased and every head turned toward her. Following a brief introduction, microphone in hand, she began to sing.

It did not take long to transform the merely listening, clapping, and humming audience into an enthusiastic, actively participating crowd. The fast rhythm and liveliness of the melodies awakened the urge to express their happy mood in movement and dance. Completely taken by the music, people jumped from their seats, gyrating energetically in one spot, jammed in between the tables, jostling each other. Nobody minded; everybody seemed to be having a good time.

In the back, the teenagers were doing their interpretation of the music in a much less enthusiastic manner, displaying restraint contrasting the abandoned enjoyment exhibited by their parents.

The dancing, singing, and drinking went on for hours. Tanya Mihailova sang and danced on the stage, accepting the applause with grace and appreciation. An older woman, seated all alone at a table abandoned by her younger companions, kept her eyes fixed on the happy, dancing crowd, occasionally wiping a tear from her smiling face.

The evening was a great success. At the end of the event most guests, still riding high waves of emotion, took a step out of their way to find the café's proprietor and express their thanks for a wonderful evening.

The man was sitting all alone at a small round table in the patio outside the café. On the chair next to him lay his briefcase. In front of him an empty, small cup of espresso sat on top of the table. He was absorbed in reading a photocopy of an article printed in a foreign newspaper that he had picked up from a pile left on the bar inside. It was the interview Tanya Mihailova had given following her return home from North America. Below the headlines in large bold letters was printed a long list of questions and answers.

## *"TANYA MIHAILVA TRIUMPHS IN NORTH AMERICA"*

*Back from a tour of Toronto, Ottawa, Montreal, New York, Chicago and Boston.*

*Q: Tanya, were you surprised, in any way, by the reception you got?*

*A: The overwhelming outpouring of love and gratitude; the warmth of the feeling of being among friends; the hugs and kisses and tears; the thanks, the flowers . . .*

*Q: Nostalgia, wouldn't you say?*

*A: How should I describe it? Let me quote, as well as I can remember the words of someone: "Thank you for taking us on a journey back to the Motherland. Thank you for bringing a breath of the fresh air of its mountains and valleys."*

*Remark of the journalist: "There are tears in your eyes. You must have been touched."*

*Tanya: "The bouquets of flowers . . ."*

The man was startled by the voice of a young woman in her twenties standing across from him. He had not heard her coming.

"Hi," she said. "Sorry I'm late . . . had to work late last night."

"Never mind," said the man as he left the newspaper on the table and stretched his arm to pick up the envelope the young woman had laid there. Pushing the photocopy toward her, he continued, "Read this while I go through the documents."

She pulled up an empty chair, sat down opposite him, and picked up the photocopy. Her eyes moved quickly from the headline down the print, then glanced over a couple of questions and answers. She pushed back the paper without finishing reading it. Clearly, she could not concentrate; her mind was occupied with other thoughts. With more than just a hint of anxiety, she inquired, "What exactly is a conditional order of departure?"

Without interrupting the examining and shuffling of papers, almost absent-mindedly, the man said, "Don't worry. It won't come to that."

He paused.

"No problem," he reassured her in a soothing voice. "Everything will be fine."

# The Benevolent Mrs. Pamela Bailey

Mr. and Mrs. Pamela Bailey lived on a short, tree-lined street in one of the most desirable locations of a big city that was famous throughout the world as diverse and tolerant—a city with a heart. And to a great degree, this reputation was well-deserved. As far as its diversity was concerned, it must be noted that the greatest factor in acquiring this reputation was its substantial immigrant population.

The street Mrs. Bailey lived on was not an exception—it had its share of immigrants. Of course, they were successful, in the material sense of the word—for, otherwise, how would they have been able to afford a home in this neighborhood? It was a very desirable one indeed. So desirable that the already heavy demand for houses kept on growing, pushing the prices higher and higher—one might say "through the roof."

Mrs. Pamela Bailey was a newcomer to the short, tree-lined street. Her preference for this location was based in part on a vague familiarity with its reputation as an exclusive area—once upon a time. It is doubtful that she was aware of the extent to which the place had changed in the last few decades, or of the character of its transformation, while still maintaining its exclusiveness—now driven strictly by affordability.

The first inkling of all that change hit her soon enough. It happened only a month or so after the Baileys moved in, when she accidentally bumped into her next-door neighbors. The encounter left her in a state of a mild shock at the discovery that, in no aspect, what-so-ever, did they fit in her social milieu expectations. Nonetheless, she was a confident, determined lady who was not easily fazed by a challenge. In this case, the solution was quite elementary: just allocate the nincompoops to the "ignore" list.

It all happened on a bright spring day, and it started in a most ordinary fashion. Mr. and Mrs. Bailey were relaxing in their living room, absorbed in reading. The pleasant ambiance and tranquility of their surroundings was further enhanced by the scent of fresh verdure and flowering bushes, by the sound of chirping birds, and by the invigorating spring breeze drifting through their open windows. That is, until a volley of loud bangs on the front door shattered the peaceful harmony. What was particularly disturbing to Mr. and Mrs. Bailey was the urgency and determination of whoever was knocking—someone so bent on getting inside their home that he did not even bother ringing the doorbell.

After a short hesitation, Mr. Bailey quickly approached the front door and swung it open. What followed left both husband and wife stunned and greatly perturbed.

A disheveled, panic-stricken woman in her late-sixties with a wild glare in her eyes and body cowering like a frightened, hunted escapee, rushed inside. Ignoring the two stupefied people standing in her way, she scurried down the hallway into the living room where she disappeared. Mr. and Mrs. Bailey were very disturbed indeed, for in this woman they did recognize one of their neighbors, Maria Valevska. Well, it was not precisely the Maria Valevska they knew, nevertheless, beyond any doubt, it was her.

It took a few moments to find Mrs. Valevska crouching between a couch and an armoire. It was obvious that she was fearful and hiding from someone or something, likely imaginary. It was also clear that it would be quite useless to try to talk her out of the state she was in, for Mrs. Valevska had completely lost her connection to reality; she had gone far away—retreated back to another time and place.

Mr. and Mrs. Bailey called an ambulance.

Meanwhile, Mr. Valevskey, a tall, neat, older man, appeared at the door. He was worried, nervous, and apologetic. Vainly he attempted to coax his wife out of her hiding place, which took the paramedics some time to achieve it.

A few hours later, Mr. Valevskey was back. He had accompanied his wife to the hospital and returned home with her. Now Mrs. Valevska was comfortably resting in their home, and her husband felt it was time for him to visit the Baileys and provide an explanation.

The Baileys were glad to learn that Mrs. Valevska was well, and frankly, this was the only thing that mattered to them. The rest of her husband's tale was quite unnecessary and they had a hard time concentrating on it—it was so irrelevant and foreign. The saga involved a country they had never heard of and a war they knew a lot about and were proud to have won. There was a young girl named Maria—Mrs. Valevska—and an occupation of the country. But there were so many occupations in the world and so much downright barbaric fighting that it was useless for the Baileys to even try to understand the entire messy situation.

Consequently to the trauma experienced during this time, Maria had developed a mental condition. She needed constant medicating, and lately her condition had gotten out of hand. Mr. Valevskey was not sure if she had been neglecting taking her pills, if the dosage had changed, or even if her condition had changed altogether.

Mr. Valevskey was very emotional and had a difficult time telling the story—his English was failing him. Throughout the entire tale the Baileys were silent—never interjecting a comment nor asking any questions. Their faces remained expressionless.

On his way out, Mr. Valevskey shook their hands—something that took the Baileys by surprise—and left with head hung between his shoulders. He felt exhausted. He had opened his heart to two strangers and now it was aching with hurt.

It seemed that this odd interlude into the daily lives of the concerned was all but forgotten—with one exception. Maria Valevska acted as though nothing had ever happened—there were no memories of the event left imprinted in her troubled mind. Mr. and Mrs. Bailey did remember it for a while, but then, since it was not something that had touched them in a profound way, they put it out of their minds. Only Mr. Valevskey was left with the aftertaste of a bad experience and had a hard time putting it out of his mind. Every time he bumped into one, or both, of the Baileys, he would stiffen up, suddenly acquiring the awkwardness of the self-conscious.

◆          ◆          ◆

A provincial election had been called and the campaign was in full swing. The white and blue signs of the PC Party, the red ones of the Liberal Party, and the orange and green ones of the NDP Party stuck in the front lawns of many of the homes throughout the neighborhood displayed the smiling, friendly faces of the candidates.

The large blue sign prominently declaring the support for the PC cause leaned precariously at the edge of the Baileys' front lawn. Completely absorbed in her task, Mrs. Bailey was struggling with both hands to straighten the tilted wooden frame. Mr. Valevskey was passing by, and, seeing the predicament Mrs. Bailey was in, jumped to her aid. Before taking his leave, Mr. Valevskey, feeling somewhat elated by his deed and wishing to show more good will toward his neighbor, inquired, "Where can I get a sign like that? I'd like to display it on our front lawn."

Caught by surprise at hearing what she considered a preposterous statement coming from someone like Mr. Valevskey, Pamela Bailey exclaimed: "PC sign?" And to make matters worse, for no particular reason, she added: "Aren't you voting NDP?"

"Why?" Mr. Valevskey snapped in an icy voice.

"Immigrants usually do. For the welfare checks and the other advantages, I suppose," the words just rolled from Pamela Bailey's mouth.

"Not all, Mrs. Bailey," he replied. "Not all. We have never asked for handouts and we have worked hard all our lives to get here," he said emphasizing his words with an expansive sweep of his arm, designating all of the surroundings. His eyes brimmed with malicious glee.

Realizing her blunder, Mrs. Bailey regained her usual composure and words of contrition poured from her lips—a bit too late for Mr. Valevskey, who had already turned his back on her and was heading toward his handsome, well-maintained house.

◆        ◆        ◆

Speaking of immigrants, it is somewhat confusing where to categorize people born outside this country but in the island that ruled it not too long ago, at least in the historical sense of time. Some of those old folks seemed to be oblivious to the fact that by now they have lost their special status and are nothing more than the rest of the newcomers. Or to be precise, this seemed to be the case with Mr. Ashton, a retired military man who lived on his own in a slightly dilapidated Victorian house—a dream property for the few developers who kept a close watch on the neighborhood's real estate potential. Clearly, though, Mr. Ashton had not the slightest intention to sell. Advanced in age, lonely, grouchy, and downright antisocial, he was not an easy man to approach, much less to be asked questions of such a sensitive nature. So the developers waited. Hopefully, his heirs would be more receptive.

A few years before the events of this story evolved, Mr. Ashton was in fairly robust health and still interested in what was happening outside the walls of his then-slightly-less-dilapidated abode. Nevertheless, he was just as mean and unfriendly as ever. His favorite pastime appeared to be spending the afternoons sitting on the front porch of his house cuddling a glass of whisky in his hands. His posture would be relaxed while his eyes would be obsessively searching the street with a steely determination—up and down, from one end to the other—trying to catch a parked vehicle. Parking was forbidden all along the tree-lined street.

The moment Mr. Ashton saw a culprit breaking the law, he would jump from his chair, rush to his telephone inside the house, and in a few minutes, the tow truck would be seen dragging the sore sight out of Mr. Ashton's view. Mr. Ashton was a stickler for the law, and he backed up his convictions with action.

◆　　　◆　　　◆

Along with the ethnic English, Italian, Caribbean, and East European immigrants, there were also another distinct group of people who, for all practical purposes, contributed to the diversity of the populace: older widows, like the venerable Mrs. Campbell.

The hardy lady of good Scottish stock, born and bred in this country, was well into her eighties. Growing feeble and her sight deteriorating, Mrs. Campbell spent most of her time indoors, all alone with her pictures and old family heirlooms. At Christmas time a few cars would be spotted moving in and out of her driveway, presumably belonging to relatives paying respects and bringing presents. However, during the rest of the year, the visits were infrequent and brief. Everybody on the street knew Mrs. Campbell as the matriarch of a well-known family, but that was all. Aloof and distant, she did not bother acknowledging even with a glance any of her neighbors when passing them on the sidewalk on her way to her hairdresser.

People did not mind. On the contrary, she seemed to bring an old flavor to the area and was a welcome sight in a place in the throes of a seemingly endless construction boom where the towering cranes never disappeared, but simply moved from one lot to another.

◆　　　◆　　　◆

A few years had passed since the Baileys moved onto the beautiful, tree-lined street.

For the residents of this peaceful neighborhood, life was blissfully free of calamities and much real excitement. There were no young children, either, to disturb the quiet. For some, it was a blessing, and for some, a drawback.

Apart from the daily routines of the folks living on the tree-lined street, one could witness extraordinary occurrences happening from time to time. And the most exciting event would be the selling of a house in the established neighborhood—the moving out of the old owners, and the moving in of the new owners. It never failed to cause a stir.

So when the "For Sale" sign appeared on the Baileys' property, there was the usual interest. But nobody was as excited as Mr. Valevskey, who had developed strong opinions about Mrs. Pamela Bailey—none of which were very flattering.

"Maria, did you noticed the sign on the Baileys front yard?" Mr. Valevskey asked his wife. "They are selling the house. Why do you think they are doing that?" he inquired, and without giving his wife a chance to respond, he continued: "Because, I tell you, these people can't stand this place anymore! They are moving north, to a 'less-diverse' place. I bet on that!"

He smirked sarcastically.

"Good riddance, I tell you! Won't miss them a bit."

Meanwhile, Mrs. Valevska had gone red in the face with agitation. She had kept her silence in embarrassment, convinced with all her heart that all that unseemly dislike for their neighbors, so deeply felt by her husband, was contrived on account of his devotion to her. It was all her fault.

In didn't take long for the house to sell. The moving vans came and left. The next day, more vans came, this time full, and left empty. The diversity on the street increased by one more ethnic entity. The Russians had arrived.

On the day the last van full with furniture turned the corner and disappeared from view, the Valevskeys went for a walk. A surreptitious glance at the now-empty Bailey house confirmed the fact that the Baileys had left. But when, exactly? Well, one would not expect that they would have said "good bye" to many. And why would they, since they hardly said "hello" to anybody when they were around?

However, this was not quite the end of the story. There had been talk among some in the neighborhood, especially after it came to be known that the Baileys had indeed moved north, to a small picturesque town by a lake—a community conspicuously lacking a diverse population. Mr. Valevskey felt vindicated.

And then, something unexpected happened. A few of the dog owners taking their beloved pets for a leisurely walk along the sidewalks of the street had been exchanging more than the usual greetings.

"The Baileys have moved—what a pity," they would say. "Pam Bailey was such a nice lady. So helpful!"

And those were not just empty words. They knew what they were talking about. Mrs. Bailey had spent many afternoons with Mrs. Campbell and a couple of other old widows, having tea, providing company and conversation, and brightening their lonely days. She had run errands for Mr. Ashton and, in general, had helped many in a variety of small and not-too-small ways. Her leaving had left a vacuum in their lives, and they missed her.

Of course the Valevskeys, the Italians, the Caribbeans, and the rest remained ignorant about Mrs. Bailey's virtues.

At the end it should be said that, in fact, Mrs. Pamela Bailey did belong to this city with a big heart. Also, it is probable that she would have never used this expression, that she likely would rather be remembered as a benevolent and charitable lady, rather than one with "a big heart." And contrary to what Mr. Valevskey thought, the Baileys did not move to escape diversity, but because of personal reasons they revealed only to Mr. and Mrs. Smyth, a couple who lived at the very end of the beautiful tree-lined street.

But then, one never knows!

# The Virtual Lives of
# Mr. Stoyanov

To say that Mr. Stoyanov enjoyed writing letters would be a gross understatement.

In order to understand his life-long dedication to this time-consuming as well as sometimes challenging activity, one should look into the motivation for doing so. His correspondence was not intended merely for maintaining old friendships or communicating with new friends and so forth, but rather to create a world apart of the one in which he lived and the perception of a life he had hoped for, but had been denied. This life was to begin when Mr. Stoyanov landed on the shores of his new country as a young DP—the official designation for "displaced person"—many years before. On his arrival from a refugee camp, he was given a few dollars and left to himself to figure out what would come next. Of course, like most refugees, he was clueless. But that was the way things were done then.

Long before he gave up on his expectations, Mr. Stoyanov had really tried to improve his chances for success. The first step he took to this end was to drop his cumbersome given name, Stoyan, and replace it with the more pleasant to the ear and easier on the tongue, Steve. It worked. Maybe in a small way, but for a lonely man, it was a welcome sign of acceptance by his peers—especially his coworkers, with whom he built roads and poured cement for sidewalks.

Their cheerful invitation of "Hey Steve, let's have a coffee!" was music to his ears. Of course, they were immigrants too. But while for some there was no difference between the few categories of newcomers—after all, they all were foreigners—the DP was at the bottom of the barrel. Or this is how they felt—or were made to feel.

For Stoyan/Steve, the loneliness never abated. This was not unexpected for a newcomer in his early twenties without much education or skills, who lacked the character traits of most of the adventurous, risk-loving, and ambitious young immigrants from the free world. For an insecure and cautious man under ordinary circumstances, Stoyan had done the unthinkable. In a single burst of determination, he had taken part in a daring escape with a couple of friends. Not many choices were left to them after what he would later consider a foolish act of joining a small political demonstration in a small provincial town. Prison, refugee camp, and all that followed did not toughen him. He merely survived, sapped of any determination or initiative after this momentous episode in his life.

Meanwhile, the thought that he would never be able to return to his birthplace—a small town where life was simple and challenges were surmountable—weighed heavily on him. And when he was given the secure job as a road maintenance worker with the city, he abandoned any notion of studying, acquiring skills, advancing, or enjoying real success. He had found his niche and felt ready to settle down in a new life, plodding along, saving and building his future toward the day he would be able to retire: like a snail moving along unhurried, carrying his protective shell.

It was also in the order of things that he should get married and raise a family. Naturally he wanted a wife from his own background, or at least a similar one.

Steve spent a couple of years in a futile search for the right girl. Women seemed to be in short supply and there was competition he could not outweigh. There was no fresh flow of newcomers from his native country, and the pool of eligible brides was small. Notwithstanding his pleasant good looks, he was deemed a rather unattractive catch, with little to offer. Among immigrants, appearance was considered secondary. In a moment of self-delusion, he even wrote to a pretty classmate in his old country and the response was enthusiastic. But in the end, he had to accept the fact that this was an impossible proposition.

Ironically, along came a nice, intelligent, and compassionate girl, a couple of generations removed from her Western European ancestors. She was completely ignorant about the place Steve had come from, and she did not show the slightest interest to learn about it. However, her partiality toward him was obvious. Growing quite discouraged in his quest of finding the right one, Steve proposed. Surprisingly, she accepted the offer to become Mrs. Stoyanov rather easily.

Her name was Linda. It did not take her long to realize that she was a consolation prize in her husband's dreams for the future. But she was a young woman with her feet firmly on the ground who recognized enough commonalities between her and Steve to make it worth sticking with him.

Theirs was not a marriage made in heaven. There were no shining moments of happiness. Mostly, it was an accommodating humdrum cohabitation. The birth of a daughter a year later cemented the relationship.

Stoyan viewed his life as comfortable and acceptably secure, though devoid of passion and excitement. But he had never looked for those things in life before, so their absence did not bother him. However, there were plenty of other things that he wished for, and that gradually filled him with disappointment and yearning.

The seeds of his future obsession with correspondence were sewn a few years earlier, by a letter he wrote on the day that he bought his first car. It was tangible proof of success, something he had never even dreamed about, and could be fully appreciated only by somebody for whom it was still as unreachable now, just as it once had been for him. He wrote to a childhood friend in a state of euphoria, with a feeling of accomplishment so new and unforgettable that he vividly remembered it in later years, and wanted to bring it back.

So he wrote another letter apologizing for not following his first one. His friend was only too glad to hear from him again and promptly responded. And from that exchange, the foundation of a correspondence that continued and accelerated throughout the years, was laid, in time developing into the hub of a network involving relatives and old friends who wrote him long, flattering letters, deprecating their own miserable lives—of course, always mindful of their government's censorship. They often asked him for advice. In his letters, Stoyan included pictures of his neat house, his shiny car parked on a highway with majestic scenery in the background, his smiling family in a park with vibrantly colored flowers in the forefront.

His letters and photos dazzled the needy, isolated small-town folk, who in return expressed their admiration for him and his success in letters filled with superlatives, praise, and awe. And if they had felt any envy toward him, it would not have bothered Stoyan at all. On the contrary, it would have increased his pleasure. To him, each letter became like a shot of aphrodisiac. He became addicted to them.

Small presents of money and old, slightly worn clothing followed, which brought him more praise and gratitude.

The family he had left behind, however, was another matter. His parents had been punished for the "betrayal" of their son and were exiled from their town to a far-away village. His younger brother, Ilia, stopped using his family name, and never tried to establish contact with his infamous brother who, in Ilia's judgment, has become nothing more than liability on his dossier.

The correspondence with his parents brought nothing but heartache to Stoyan. One day he received a letter from a neighbor telling him that his mother had followed his deceased father. Stoyan collected all of his parents' letters, including the one he had just received informing him of his mother's passing, secured the bunch with a rubber band and placed them in the bottom drawer of his small desk.

The years rolled by in a world suspended in a timeless state of fear and distrust between the people living on both sides of an impenetrable divide. And there was no end in sight. Stoyan's innocuous life was running its course without many bumps or shakes along the way. Linda was comfortably settled into her life filled with work and caring for their daughter, Mary. The girl was growing pretty and smart, providing her father with still more good news to brag about in his voluminous letters. Along with pictures of his daughter, he would send photocopies of her end-of-term school reports, accompanied by a translation. In return, he received letters glowing with admiration for Mary, and only in passing would anyone mention their own children, instead sticking to the overall tone of sorry tales about their own lives filled with problems and hopelessness. Stoyan would send them some more money and old clothes.

At some point in time, a new name had been added to the list of correspondents. Velko was a distant cousin who initiated contact after seeing pictures and hearing passages from Stoyan's letters passed along by mutual kinfolk. After a slight hesitation, the relatives eventually had supplied Velko with their now-famous relative's address. A couple of weeks later, a long letter with an unfamiliar return address was delivered to Stoyan's home.

Stoyan was pleased enormously. The touching warmth and adroitly expressed humility brought tears to his eyes. He simply could not put down this testament of affection and admiration, and read it over and over. Needless to say, it was the beginning of an intense correspondence. Velko's letters were the most satisfying, transcending the ordinary naive flattery and the not-too-subtle supplicant tone of the rest. Unquestionably, Velko was a master of the written word.

When Velko expressed a desire to come and visit, Stoyan was overwhelmed with excitement. His concern that travel was almost impossible was soothed by his cousin; he conveyed a message assuring him that there was no problem in this regard. However, there was the small matter with the ticket: he could not afford it. It was up to Stoyan to take the initiative.

In front of the sliding doors separating the enclosed arrival area from the wide entrance hall of the airport terminal, along a cordoned pathway, a stream of passengers were advancing slowly, pushing carts overflowing with luggage. The weary, slightly bewildered travelers were met by throngs of waving relatives and friends. On the edge of the crowd stood Stoyan, anxiously trying to discern a familiar figure among the middle-aged men passing through the gates.

As if from nowhere, a slender, average-height man appeared only a few feet away from him, fast approaching with a determined, quick step and smiling, shifty eyes set in a tawny, sun-burned, weasel-like face. Momentarily, he halted in front of Stoyan, let his suitcase drop on the carpet-covered floor and threw his arms around his cousin in a tight embrace. He burst into a torrent of words.

"Brother! Brother! Finally to meet again!" he sputtered. "Can't believe it! What a moment! A dream come true!"

Tears of joy were streaming from his eyes, rolling down his cheeks, dropping on his jacket. Smiling, with misty eyes, Stoyan just stood there, occasionally letting a giggle escape his tensed throat all while continuously landing comforting taps on his cousin's back.

Over the next few days, the two cousins spent most of their time inside the sparsely furnished living room of Stoyan's home, mostly alone, reminiscing about old times and catching up with the present. The communications were largely one-sided. Velko did the talking and Stoyan the listening, seemingly never tiring from doing so. Finally, under the urging of his wife, Stoyan decided to take his guest on a few short sightseeing trips. Surprisingly, though, Velko did not seem to be as interested in the experience. Hardly able to keep his attention away from the conversation, his curiosity seemed easily satisfied with no more than a perfunctory glance at the scenery outside the car window. Clearly, his mind was somewhere else.

Meanwhile, Stoyan was having the time of his life.

A couple of weeks elapsed. During the last few days of his visit, Velko started to show signs of restlessness. Carefully he had made it clear that he had come just to see his favorite cousin and now, having achieved his goal in a marvelous way, he was ready to head back home. The family back home would have a hard time managing without him, he said—especially his son. Apparently, the lad had a big problem, although from Stoyan's standpoint, an unusual one for a man living in a state of permanent want for almost all of life's necessities. The young man needed a car, and his father felt strongly that his place was to be close to his son in his time of need.

Increasingly, Velko's tirades acquired the dark and dispirited tones of lamentation. Steve's reaction was to the point.

"Brother, how much money do you need for a car?" he asked his cousin.

"Never mind, brother," Velko replied. "It is my problem. I came here merely to see you and this is the most joyous time in my life. Let us drop the subject."

A few moments later, he added, "I am sorry to have bothered you with my problems, but the worry never goes away. It is hard for you to understand. Let's not talk about it anymore."

Steve was deeply touched.

"But I could help you, brother," Steve said. "Just let me!"

By the end of the third week, Velko was on his way back home. The two cousins parted at the airport in a hurry. All smiles, Velko warmly hugged his cousin, who stood rigid and crestfallen before him, then energetically grabbed Stoyan's limp hand and squeezed it firmly between the palms of his hands.

"I'll never forget your kindness to me and my son, brother," Velko said.

And with these last words, looking straight ahead, Velko sprightly entered the departure area to wait for his flight.

The correspondences between the two cousins continued, only less frequently and diminished in intensity. At times Velko's letters were downright sloppy.

However, at least in one regard, this visit was the catalyst for a change in Stoyan's ambiguous attitudes toward his native country. He had experienced a new sense of reconnecting with the past. The notion that at some point in time, as indefinite as it might be, he would return to visit his homeland became a possibility not to be discounted. At times, he pondered even the proposition that maybe his place was there. He had friends there who liked, accepted, and appreciated him.

And as history would have it, a few years later, to the utter surprise of most, this became a real possibility. Well, not exactly. It took a few more years for Stoyan to overcome his long-nursed suspicions and gain enough confidence to brave the unknown—a journey back home—until it became inevitable.

Meanwhile, he had received news from his brother. Somehow Ilia had managed to get on with his life quite successfully, acquiring a university education in the field of law. He had married, landed a good job, and settled in a big city with his family. Stoyan was surprised and relieved that he had no cause to feel guilty about bringing harm to his little brother's future. It would be nice to see Ilia. Besides, since his recent retirement, he had all the free time he needed to spend in any fashion he wished, and while on one hand the slight problems he was experiencing with his health had a deterring effect on his decision, on the other hand they added to the urgency to go before he reached an advanced age or his health became an impediment to his travel plans.

In the crowded terminal of a small, run-down airport, Steve and Ilia came face to face, hardly able to recognize each other and lost for words. Releasing his younger sibling from an awkward embrace, Stoyan turned to his pretty sister-in-law, accepted a bouquet of flowers from her hands, and placed an even more awkward peck on her cheek.

The next few days passed in an atmosphere of unease—without bringing the estranged siblings any closer to each other. As a lawyer, a profession that had emerged from a state of irrelevance in the old times to a lucrative occupation in the new ones, Ilia exuded confidence that went along well with his comfortable lifestyle—not free from worry, but more than acceptable measured against the background of the country's standard. Indeed, Stoyan felt a small pang of envy and became rather eager to escape the feeling by getting in touch with his long-time pen pals, especially with Velko, as soon as possible.

His brother did his best to make Stoyan's stay pleasant, taking him first to the small town where they were born and to their parents' grave, where both shed tears, and for a fleeting moment felt close, sharing their sorrow. Then Ilia took his brother around the country. Stoyan genuinely liked much of what he saw, but strangely, instead of gladness and exhilaration, he felt overwhelmed by complex feelings that left him in a state of exhaustion and anxiety. He had enough of picturesque seashore panoramas drenched in sunshine, of forest-covered mountains that harbored quaint old monasteries and churches with walls covered in frescoes of saints with gaunt faces and stern eyes.

"Everything is old," he remarked with a hint of disappointment.

"That is the point," Ilia retorted, irritated by the lack of appreciation in his older brother.

He decided to cut the trip short.

Back at the apartment, Ilia's wife got busy making calls, arranging visits to Stoyan's friends. And eventually, the long anticipated invitation from Velko came.

On the appointed day, an hour later than the designated time, a freshly washed German car, only a couple of years old, with stickers on its bumper indicating the Western European country where its previous owner had resided, came to a stop in front of Ilia's apartment building. Velko, accompanied by a heavy, though quite agile young man, emerged from the vehicle.

The two cousins greeted each other warmly. Velko introduced the young man as his son, Rumen, and after a brief visit with Ilia's family, he took Stoyan for a visit to his home in a town some eighty kilometers away. At the end of a pleasant drive along a road winding through a hilly countryside, the car came to a stop in front of a two-story whitewashed house surrounded by a smart-looking stone and iron fence. A flagstone-covered path lined with rows of splendid rose bushes in full bloom led to the front door. Behind the house, a patch of delicate string beans tied around thin poles suggested the existence of a neat vegetable garden.

To the eyes of the average tourist this small, unpretentious house probably would be no more than a pleasant picture of a tranquil, sedate life in a small town. To Stoyan, though, it was much more than that: it was a warm and happy place. And when Velko's son did not follow them through the open gate, he almost wishfully inquired, "This is not your house, is it?"

"Oh, yes," Velko replied. "This is mine and my old lady's place. The young ones have their own place, bigger and new, a little farther down the street. This one is smaller and more peaceful. We hope you will like it here."

Indeed, Stoyan liked it. It would be fair to say that he liked it a bit too much.

That night, lying between the crisp, freshly sun-dried sheets in the small neat room, Stoyan could not chase away the tormenting thoughts that made his head pound and his body toss restlessly in bed.

The next day he became even more irritable. He started asking all kinds of questions, demanding answers.

"Is this the car Rumen bought with the money I gave you?" he asked. "This is one fancy car he got. And a new, big house you said?"

For a moment Velko seemed at a loss for words.

"The car? That old wreck?" he replied. "He sold it a few years ago. This one he bought only last year. The house is new also, yes. Rumen is very enterprising. He has a business now—import-export."

He paused to add a meaningful sigh,

"Without your help, though, it would have been impossible to make it."

For Stoyan, however, it was too little, too late. By then he was in a state of constant anxiety, even physically ill from tiredness due to inability to relax and get a good night's rest. The end of his stay came not a minute too soon.

He was ready to head back home. As a matter of fact, the images of the past few days preceding his departure were a blur leaving no clear imprint in his memory. The telephone calls from his pen pals bidding him farewell and wishing him a good trip back, the partings, the last dinner in a new fancy restaurant with Ilia and his wife—it all seemed to be happening to somebody else.

With his hands shaking and his voice rising to a screeching high pitch, hardly able to concentrate on a single task, he collected his clothes and souvenirs, hurriedly stuffing them in the suitcase.

After one last look at the quickly receding landscape below the ascending airplane, Stoyan pulled down the blind over the window by his seat and let out a sigh of relief. It was good to be homebound.

Somewhere over the Atlantic, far from land to the east and to the west, a frazzled stewardess ran to the purser of the flight.

"Doctor, please," she cried. "The passenger in seat 32A fainted."

The patient was examined by a doctor aboard the plane who in his preliminary evaluation concluded that the passenger had suffered a stroke. Mr. Stoyanov was given the best possible care under the circumstances, and a distress call was sent ahead to the authorities on the ground.

On the tarmac, near the landing area for the oncoming planes, an ambulance and its crew stood by in anticipation for the arrival of the sick passenger. As soon as the aircraft came to a stop, the paramedics rushed toward it. Without delay, Mr. Stoyanov was transferred to the waiting vehicle and whisked away to a hospital. Inside the ambulance, he lay with his eyes closed and his hand resting in his wife Linda's cool palms, listening to her soothing voice that was drowned out at times by the piercing sound of the siren.

"How lucky you did not fall ill before you left," she said. "Who knows what kind of hospitals and what care is available over there?"

After a few days, Mr. Stoyanov was released from the hospital. His condition was assessed as good but for a slight paralysis on the left side of his face. The doctors' consensus opinion, though, was that the damage was not irreversible, and in time, with the help of additional therapy, a complete recovery was possible. During his hospital stay, his daughter, Mary, had brought along her boyfriend, Tony, on one of her visits. On the day of his discharge, Mr. Stoyanov learned they had decided to get married. The timing for breaking the news was a way to cheer him up and have a positive influence on the process of full recuperation ahead of him.

"Are you pleased, Steve?" Linda had inquired when left alone with her husband.

Pleased? Steve was hesitating. He had never thought about anything in those terms. Had she, or anyone, for that matter, ever been concerned about pleasing or displeasing him?

"Yes, I am pleased," he said finally while looking at his wife's once fresh, pretty face now looking prematurely aged—its features heavy, the contour lines of its once delicate oval, now distorted by flabby skin and sagging jowls.

*She looks old.* A mental note, no more than an indifferent observation, flashed through his mind.

◆      ◆      ◆

Mary Stoyanov and Anthony Peske were married in a moving ceremony performed in an old stone church on a pleasant autumn afternoon. Contrary to the impression suggested by the solemn distinction of the building of an old-fashioned wedding, the ceremony was far from traditional and went against the secret desires of both sets of parents.

The service was conducted by a female minister from The United Church of Canada. Needless to say, neither the bride nor groom was raised in its traditions, and most of their guests were not, either. But aside from this one small wrinkle, the perfectly planned event went smoothly. Both young and old guests expressed their delight with the beautiful bride and handsome groom, the entire wedding party, the reception in the tastefully decorated bright hall, and the entertainment provided by a live orchestra.

The food had been served and the music was playing. The laughter and the thud of stamping feet on the dancing floor had reached its crescendo. It looked like everybody was having a great time.

A plump, middle-aged woman stood next to a table, enthusiastically clapping as her eyes followed the dancing couples twirling under the irresistible rhythm of the tarantella dance.

"Great party!" she said. "I love Italian weddings."

"Absolutely! Italians know how to celebrate," replied another middle-aged plump woman dressed in a well-made outfit following the latest fashion.

"The bride is not Italian, is she?" the first lady said. "Has an unusual family name. Stoyonow, or something like that," added the first lady.

"It doesn't matter now, though. She just changed it, didn't she?" the well-dressed one said with a smile. Then, pointing toward a nearby table occupied by a middle-aged couple, she continued,

"I believe that those are the parents of the bride, Linda and Steve Stoyanov. Never met them."

Both women let their eyes linger at the sight. The woman at the table was seated comfortably in her chair, looking relaxed and quietly happy. The man sat stiffly some distance away from the table with his arms crossed in front of his chest, observing the scene with a detached stare and a half-smirk—an impression created by the frozen, partially distorted left side of his face.

"Hmm . . . Linda and Steve? Canadians, I suppose. Nice people!" the first lady said absentmindedly.

Then suddenly losing interest in the lonely couple, she turned her eyes back to the dance floor and resumed clapping with an increased vigor, keeping up with the quickening tempo of the music.

# *Resume of an Engineer*

Mrs. Olga Tomov was one of those lucky people who enjoyed their work. It did not start that way; the job kind of grew on her.

She never thought that she would end up teaching. In fact, she had never even contemplated the possibility until she got tired of her battle to make a career out of her field of expertise: she was an engineer, and a mechanical one to boot.

But let us rewind the tape and go back to the beginning.

◆          ◆          ◆

### Chasing the elusive Canadian experience; librarians, draft-dodgers, and the strange interview with Mr. Shepherd

It was the sixties when Olga first came to Canada, and it didn't take long before she realized that she was viewed as an exception, a sort of a curiosity, as far as her chosen line of work was concerned. Things were different in the place she came from: women were entering all the professions and were led to believe that the playing field was level. Like most, Olga became disillusioned quickly. She thought it would be different in the West. However, it did not turn out that way.

In the mid-sixties, jobs were plentiful. Typically, it took only a few applications to get an interview that led to an offer. After sending countless letters and receiving nothing more than acknowledgments, Olga's optimism started to dwindle while her apprehension grew. Not a single interview.

She almost had one, but in the final analysis, the letter was not to be counted since it was addressed to *Mr.* Tomov—clearly a misunderstanding that resulted from the lack of familiarity with foreign names, or some such thing, not quite clear to her. The letter read:

*Dear Mr. Tomov:*

*We are very pleased to have your letter in response to our ad for the position of Mechanical Engineer. We are enclosing one of our regular application forms which we would ask that you complete and return to us.*

*We are planning to hold interviews with applicants in the near future. No date has been set yet, but we will contact you and arrange a time most convenient for both of us.*

*Very truly yours,*
*(signature)*

As requested, Olga completed the application and returned it, full of hope and anticipation—sentiments, which slowly diminished with each passing day till, finally, evaporated entirely.

The rejection letters kept coming. She started sorting them out and filing them into piles under different headings. There were a few more letters addressed to *Mr.* Tomov, and they sounded rather nice, containing passages like:

*We have carefully reviewed your background and experience which are certainly extensive. However, we do not feel that the requirements of the position we have to offer would match your qualifications to our mutual advantage.*

Well, it *was* a rejection, but the reference to her "background and experience" made her feel appreciated. Maybe foolish, nevertheless, a comforting thought that let her imagine her rejection was only partial.

On the other hand, the letters to Mrs. Tomov were more polite, even consolatory.

*Dear Mrs. Tomov,*
*The position of mechanical draftsman, for which you recently applied, has been filled.*

*I hope you will not mind if we keep your application and resume on file in case there is another opening in our office.*

For the time being, Olga had abandoned her hope of finding a position as an engineer and began to apply for any technical job. Meanwhile, she tried to register with the Association of Professional Engineers, but that was not easy, either; only a handful of women were registered—none from Eastern Europe. To complicate matters even further, there were none, neither male of female, from her alma mater. The administrator of the association indicated that lack of precedent stood in the way of evaluating her academic qualifications.

The lack of *Canadian experience*, though, appeared to be the greatest of all obstacles in finding employment at any level. And when the pile of letters rejecting her for that reason alone grew high enough to warrant special attention, she created a category in her files under the heading "The vicious circle."

So she decided that the best course of action would be to find *any* job for the sole purpose of satisfying that particular requirement.

Olga found a part-time job as a library assistant at the University of T, doing filing work for ten hours a week. In one respect, this was a fortunate event, an eye-opener really, for there she found out that her situation was not unique. Ninety-nine percent of the people working in the department were in situations similar to hers: a lawyer from Italy, a French professor from Egypt, a medical doctor from Poland (who was in the process of taking some kind of qualifying exams), and many others who had no hope of ever being accredited within their fields of study. All these professionals had received their education outside the country, and many had been given a high number of points on that account, which boosted their chances of being accepted as immigrants.

The department had about fifty employees and was run very efficiently by Mrs. Vecmanis, a fair woman with blue eyes and blond hair that she wore in a chignon. She dressed in elegant, well-made clothes, and her coiffure was impeccable—there was not a strand of hair out of place. Her poise and professionalism evoked respect.

Nevertheless, the overriding impression she gave was that of an almost tragic figure, wrapped in a shroud of sorrow.

Only a couple of weeks into her job, Olga was called into the boss's office. Completely ignorant of the reason for the unexpected attention, her palms were sweating and her heart was fluttering as she took the seat opposite the formidable Mrs. Vecmanis.

After a brief interval of silence, Mrs. Vecmanis began.

"Olga, you remind me so much of myself when I first came to Canada over twenty years ago. I know how you feel. I used to be an opera singer back home, married with two small children. My husband was a journalist. He was sent to

Siberia by the Russians. I never heard from him and at the end of the war came to Canada alone with the children. As I mentioned, I was an opera singer . . ."

Her voice trailed into silence again.

"Maybe you will succeed and find work as an engineer," she continued. "Meanwhile, would you like a full-time job as a library assistant?"

Olga's eyes grew big as saucers and gleamed with tears she was trying to keep from rolling down her cheeks. Overwhelmed by feelings she could not express in her limited English, she muttered a few words of gratitude and left the office in a hurry, sure that Mrs. Vecmanis would not have liked any show of weakness.

Back home, Olga pulled out her resume and added,

> *November 1966-present:*
> *Library Assistant, University of T., Canada*

It was a start!

It didn't take much time to learn the job. She quickly became familiar with the volumes of Library of Congress catalogues; with the routine of searching titles, authors, references, and catalogue numbers. The environment was pleasant, bright, and quiet.

Olga spent hours standing by stalls a few meters long and covered with catalogues and books, shoulder to shoulder with her coworkers, who came from all over the world. Some had come in search of a better life, and some simply found themselves here: forced out of their countries by political turbulence, wars, or economic hardship—like debris deposited by a storm on the ocean shore. Next to the West Germans, Dutch, Italian, Swedish, and Finnish immigrants stood the old Russian and Ukrainian refugees from the October revolution of 1917. There were the Latvian, Lithuanian, and Estonian runaways from the Soviet Union at the end of the Second World War, which included Mrs. Vecmanis, the head of the department. There were recent Egyptian immigrants who had been forced out by the Nasser regime, and the few Eastern Europeans who had managed to escape out from under the Iron Curtain. And there were the young, somewhat bewildered American draft-dodgers. Most were educated, intelligent, and planning for a future that did not include their present occupation.

For the inquisitive at heart, it was a great place to be for a while. At least this is how Olga viewed her situation. Encountering so many different cultures and points of view—some so alien to hers—was a revelation. Even the couple of Canadians who worked in the library were of a temperament more akin to this multinational crowd.

The first person to befriend Olga was Carol, a Canadian from Saskatchewan. Her ancestry was a mixture of German, Ukrainian, and a few other nationalities she was only vaguely aware of. A year after they had met at the library, Carol was off to Australia in search of a new home. For several years, they kept in touch, until Carol wrote that she was moving to the interior. It sounded very adventurous.

Olga never heard from her again.

Meanwhile, a kind of mini-explosion of babies born to the numerous female employees occurred in the department. Olga had her baby, too—a girl. The new mother was overwhelmed by the large number of flowers and presents sent her in the hospital by her coworkers. The enormous bouquet of roses was particularly touching, since they were her favorite flowers. The silver cup and greeting card from Mrs. Vecmanis signed "with affection" brought tears to her eyes, and the enormous congratulatory card covered with almost fifty signatures was impressive.

According to a rumor, there were more than sixty different languages spoken by the vastly diverse group of library assistants employed by the university. That richness of linguistic skills was a source of pride for the entire department, and everybody seemed eager to demonstrate those skills whenever the occasion presented itself. It was customary for everyone to express their "best wishes" in their mother tongue and only their signatures in English. Needless to say, nobody could read them all, so one had to trust that what they wrote were expressions of well-meant thoughts.

It was springtime. First, it was the grass that came alive again, its strong, dark green blades pushing up through the moist earth. Then forsythia shrubs bloomed, with their bright-yellow flowers, then daffodils and tulips. And, finally, the delicate new tree leaves transformed the landscape once dominated by the shades of dark brown tree trunks and branches and piles of dirty snow and ice sticking to the roadsides.

Sunshine flooded the large room. The rows of desks by the windows were awash with its brilliant light. At the very back of the room, where the walls were covered with bookshelves from floor to ceiling, only a few people were standing by the tables. Except for the sounds of flipping pages and scratching pens, it was quiet.

Suddenly, a cry of anguish, followed by a torrent of confused, incomprehensible words, burst out from the shadows, shattering the silence. Heads turned, eyes shifted toward the back. There, Anna—the Polish doctor—stood among papers and books strewn on the floor around her feet, her body shaking violently, her eyes fixed in space, and her lips spewing words directed to no one and everyone at once.

Only the refrain, "I can't stand it! I can't take it anymore," heard in intervals, was intelligible.

A few people rushed and took hold of her, pulling her into one of the small offices, muttering words of comfort, trying to calm her down. She did not resist, but her wailing and moaning could be heard throughout the floor until she disappeared behind the closed office door. Shortly after, the piercing sound of a siren announced the departure of an ambulance, and everybody settled back to work in silence, heavy with uneasiness. Before the work day was over, news came from the hospital: Anna was to remain there for an indefinite period. She had suffered a nervous breakdown.

Olga decided that it was time to start looking for a new job.

Her resume went back in circulation.

This time, though, she approached the search with new confidence, for her English had improved considerably. Still, it was going to be difficult; a change of strategy and new avenues for finding job opportunities were needed. The specialized employment agencies seemed promising, especially the one affiliated to the Association of Professional Engineers. She contacted them and arranged an interview for a month later. It happened to fall on her birthday.

*This is a good omen*, she kept thinking. Moreover, it was her first interview, so she felt a heightened sense of anticipation and excitement.

On the day of the interview, she put on her best clothes and arranged her hair with particular care. She even wore some makeup—something she almost never did. Her husband was to accompany her for moral support—in case her English faltered and to steady her if she became too emotional.

Inside a nice office, a pleasant man named Mr. Shepherd met them with a broad smile and a firm handshake. He comported himself in a friendly and easy manner, looking at Mr. and Mrs. Tomov, who were seated opposite him at the large desk, shifting his glance from one to the other as he spoke in a display of charming politeness, as well as in a deliberate effort to bestow even-handed attention toward each.

"So, Mrs. Tomov, you are an engineer," he began. "How very interesting. What made you go into engineering?"

It was a question that was put to her many times in later years, and by then she had formulated a well-rehearsed answer. But hearing it for the first time, she was stunned. *Why*, really? She had never thought about it, and now she was lost for words.

"I enjoyed physics and mathematics. Besides, it was not unusual, so . . ." her answer trailed into a mutter.

"You are employed at the moment, yes?" Mr. Shepherd asked.

"Yes, as a library assistant."

"Mr. Tomov, you are employed also?"

"Yes, I am," Mr. Tomov replied quickly.

He was relaxed and eager to help. Mr. Tomov had never had problems finding employment. The couple of jobs he had after graduating from an American university came easily.

Mr. Shepherd paused for a moment, apparently pondering what he had just been told.

"So what is the problem?" he asked." You are such a young, nice-looking couple, and are both employed. Library assistant is not a bad job for a woman, is it?"

By then, Mrs. Tomov had regained her composure.

"Mr. Shepherd, I am an engineer, and I would like to work as an engineer," she said confidently.

"Well, yes, of course. Are you willing to relocate?"

"Yes, I am."

"Yes, we are," Mr. Tomov added in response to the inquiring look Mr. Shepherd had sent in his direction.

"Very well, then," Mr. Shepherd said as he stood up, indicating the interview was over. "We will see what we can do."

"You have a resume?" he asked. "Thank you."

Mr. Shepherd stretched his left arm to accept the papers proffered him over the desk by Mrs. Tomov while offering his right hand for another firm handshake.

Outside the office, Mrs. Tomov suddenly felt annoyed with her elegantly knitted, pale blue manteau, high heels, and stylish hairdo. Mr. Tomov wore a sour expression on his face.

"He did not inquire about my experience," Olga said, referring to her engineering experience.

"No, he did not," her husband said. "But at least he took your resume."

Neither felt like celebrating. The next birthday, maybe.

A number of American draft-dodgers worked at the library. Naturally, they were all men, but there were also a few women who had moved to Canada for various reasons as well. Most had simply followed their boyfriends into their self-imposed exile.

One day, a tall, blond girl, originally from Ohio and single at the time, stirred quite a bit of excitement when she appeared at work on crutches. Both of her legs were injured—one was in a cast, the other one in bandages. Her arms and head also showed signs of physical trauma. She was moving with great difficulty and was advancing slowly toward her desk. She had been absent for a while and rumor had it that she was in a hospital after jumping from a window in a state of euphoria during an LSD trip, convinced that she could fly. Fortunately, she landed on a soft patch of grass and survived, but just barely.

There were no words of sympathy for the poor girl who had almost killed herself. For the majority of the employees, her behavior was incomprehensible. Olga heard nothing but derision regarding the incident but, moved by compassion and bewilderment, tried to understand. That led to a few brief friendships with some of the American exiles. Brief for no other reason that they did not stick around for long; they were restless people in transition.

So with her husband and their baby, Olga attended a hippie wedding in the park, joined a rally on the streets, listened to their ballads, and at times was moved to tears. But the message never got to her.

However, the image of the rebels was irresistible. Feeling rejected, she fell, if not for the idea, at least for the image of the hippie. Out went the pale-blue knitted manteau, the high-heel shoes, the cute dresses, and fashionable haircuts, replaced by the simple look of homemade garb and straight, long hair.

Meanwhile, the rejection letters kept coming and, to her great annoyance, even more than before were addressed to Mr. Tomov. Things must have been getting tougher in the job market, she reasoned. Two years went by without an interview. Then she received a call from a technical services agency about a position for a draftsperson in a small electronics company.

A stocky and energetic man, Mr. Greg Baker, interviewed her. He frankly admitted that his interest in Mrs. Tomov was due partially to the favorable impression he had of a draftswoman employed by one of his business clients. He did not reveal to her that her gender played an even more significant role in his considerations: the company was in a process of developing a new product, a movie camera, and Mr. Baker had more faith in the artistic abilities of women. He was convinced that Mrs. Tomov was exactly the person he needed for the design of the exterior of the camera.

When Olga was extended a job offer, she became euphoric. The fact that she knew nothing about electronics did not fluster her at all. On the other hand, giving notice to Mrs. Vecmanis was not an easy thing to do.

Olga's farewell party at the library was a happy, cheerful event. Mrs. Vecmanis was all smiles. Olga was presented with a handsome letter case and an oversized card covered with signatures and well-wishes expressed in more than twenty different languages.

The very next day, Olga started her new job. She got up very early, dressed in a hurry, and said good-bye to her husband and daughter. In a state of nervous excitement, she left the house clutching a note with instructions on how to get to her new workplace. The trip involved changing two busses and a ride on the subway.

For the next four years, she would be commuting along this same route.

◆          ◆          ◆

### On beautiful friendships, the ups and downs of "growing wings", and the ugly movie camera

ABC Electronics was a small company with about fifteen employees—no big departments, and few managers. Besides Mr. Baker, there was Mr. Robert Chepelsky, the president of the company, who spent most of his time hidden away in his enormous office, emerging occasionally when giving a tour to a client. There were no manuals and no employee job descriptions, and everybody had to do a variety of tasks.

Olga did all the drafting, designed housing for audio and video systems, drilled holes on PC boards, and soldered the components that fit inside them. She even learned how to design the boards.

The company was something of a family enterprise; a couple of the president's siblings worked there, but more importantly, it functioned like a family. The petty jealousies, gossip, and politics were no different from those of a large company, but here they were more personal. With the exception of Olga, all employees had been born in the country, and no one involved in the engineering side of the business had a university degree. Instead, they were a bunch of enterprising, capable, no-nonsense men, dedicated to the constant search for opportunities to make money.

It was hardly the place for someone like her to grow and advance, Olga pondered. Yet, at least for the time being, she was content. Most of the people were amiable and easy to get along with.

She made a few friends.

One of them was Danny, a Jehovah's Witness and a clerk in the shipping department. He was a reformed person who had found the strength to change his bad ways of the past and to start a new life thanks to his new religion. Convinced that his experience was miraculous, now he wanted to help others—earnestly and relentlessly—to see the truth as he had seen it. He used every opportunity—during his lunch hour or on his afternoon break—to hand out literature to Olga and to expound on his beliefs.

Olga tried to explain to him that she was not desperate and her problems had nothing to do with the bigger things in life. She assured him that her soul was at peace. But Danny would not have it. Eventually, he had to give up on her, and that was the end of their friendship. However, he kept on letting her know that she had her chance for salvation and she had missed it, occasionally darting quick glances in her direction full of sadness and disappointment.

And then there was Georgia, a vivacious, attractive woman who moved with a gait that made men turn their heads and follow her with eyes full of appreciation. She owned a red convertible sports car, which she drove like crazy, with the top down—weather permitting. Georgia was Mr. Chepelsky's secretary. She was very efficient and hardworking. She seldom left her desk, located in front of her boss's door, but her loud, obnoxious bursts of laughter could frequently be heard throughout the place.

Olga was attracted to Georgia's free-spirited ways, and Georgia—often the object of petty jealousy and envy from the other women in the office—found Olga's different outlook on life interesting. For a change, Olga's accent and odd occupation paid a dividend.

"You are an engineer? What a strange bird you are!" Georgia laughed in amusement.

In Olga's opinion, one of the most important attributes people could have was a "good heart." Georgia absolutely fell into this category, but this was not the case with Georgia's father, whom Olga met once.

Georgia lived with her parents, not far from work. Sometimes she would take Olga along to her house for lunch. There, her mother would serve them soup and sandwiches, which they would eat in front of the television set. Georgia would be engrossed in a soap opera she watched faithfully whenever she had the chance, and Olga would absorb herself in a conversation with Georgia's mother.

On one of those lunchtime visits, the tranquility of the setting was suddenly disturbed by the sound of a banging door. Georgia and her mother fell into complete silence and, for a fleeting moment, the room was filled with uneasiness. The noise was followed by the appearance of a tall, heavy-set, older man. As he entered, he stopped at the door with a look of slight surprise. It was Mr. Hughes, Georgia's father. Without bothering to wait for the end of his wife's introduction of Olga, he turned around and walked out of the room.

On their way back to work, speeding along the streets, Georgia remarked casually with a smile on her face, "Don't pay attention to my dad. He is a bigot. He does not like immigrants."

"But you are not like that at all," Olga said. "You have 'the typical social grace of a Canadian,' as Hemmingway put it."

A loud squeal came from the driver's side. With her right hand on the steering wheel and her left arm resting on the open window frame, Georgia shouted between peals of laughter while accelerating the car even more.

"Where did Hemmingway write that?" Georgia asked, still laughing.

"I don't remember. Must have read it a long time ago," Olga shouted back.

The visits to Georgia's house continued. Occasionally, Olga would hear the front door opening and feel a surge of anxiety, but Mr. Hughes never came into the room and she never saw him again.

At the end of the first year at ABC Electronics, Olga became a member of the professional engineering association. She had fulfilled the requirement of one year of Canadian experience set as a prerequisite for her acceptance.

In the summer of 1970, a letter addressed to the association and signed by R. Norton, P.Eng. stated that:

> *"Mrs. Tomov had just completed one year as a member of the engineering department at ABC Electronics. I understand that she has been most helpful and thorough in solving their mechanical problems. Any consideration and assistance to Mrs. Tomov in her endeavor to become registered with the Association of Professional Engineers will be truly appreciated."*

Six months later, Olga received a letter from the association addressed to Mrs. O. Tomov, P. Eng. There was no need to read any further. She felt as if she had grown wings.

Then she read the letter, not once but many times, combing through the text, ascribing a special meaning to each phrase and every word.

> *Dear Mrs. Tomov,*
>     *It is my pleasure to inform you that . . . etc.* (a pleasure!). *On behalf of the President and members of Council, I wish you success* (I wish you!) *in the practice of your profession.*
> *Yours truly,*

"I am *in*!"

Soon after this truly momentous event in Olga's life, an event that boosted her confidence and lifted her spirits, the prototype of the new camera housing was brought from the machine shop. The clumsy, dull contraption made of sheet metal resembled an oversized mailbox. Only by a great leap of the imagination could one have associated such an object with a movie camera; it was unimaginable that anybody would feel proud of designing such a thing. Olga was brought down to earth and felt more than a tinge of guilt. She had let down Mr. Baker—any man could have done as badly as she had.

Maybe it was time to start searching for a new job. For now, though, she decided to stay, for she felt bound by a feeling of gratitude toward her boss, Greg Baker. Nevertheless, she took out the resume and updated the last entry:

> *November 1966-July 1969:*
> *Assistant Librarian.*
> *In 1969 I left the library to pursue a career in my professional field.*

> *July 1969-present: ABC Electronics*
> *Draftswoman,*
> *Duties:*

Adding a completely new entry:

*Professional memberships:*
*Association of Professional Engineers (January 1971).*

Ten months later, a new cycle of applying and dealing with rejection began.

As before, some of the acknowledgement letters were addressed to *Mr.* Tomov; only now, the designation of P. Eng had been attached to the name; whereas the ones addressed to Mrs. Tomov seldom had it. The former often promised an interview, but as soon she let them know that they were dealing with Mrs. rather Mr., there was no follow-up.

Before closing that chapter in Mrs. Tomov's professional life, another significant event occurred, one that started her on the road to becoming something of a nuisance to all kind of authorities. Maybe the title of P. Eng. went to her head, but after the incident, emboldened by the status of recognition as a professional engineer, or simply fed up with frustration, she hardly missed a chance to make a fuss—"to fight for her rights," as she would put it.

The Tomov family was relaxing after dinner in front of the television set one evening when the phone rang. The call was for Mrs. Tomov and it was regarding a job in an institute, a place she had never heard of, and regarding a position she had never applied for. The institute's staff was almost exclusively comprised of females. They needed an engineer and had asked the Association of Professional Engineers to recommend a woman for the job. It was an unusual request; nevertheless, it was true.

The association had submitted Mrs. Tomov's name and provided the caller with information on her background, education, and experience. The caller indicated that he was satisfied with her qualifications and that she met all requirements for the position. In short, it was up to her.

He gave her a brief description of the job and was eager to see her as soon as possible to discuss salary and to give her a tour of the premises, and, if she agreed to the conditions, to sign some papers. At the end of the conversation, it sounded like a done deal. For the first time ever, Olga felt courted and wanted. Four weeks' vacation, excellent location, personal secretary . . . it all sounded so good!

The next day, still slightly giddy with excitement, Mrs. Tomov showed up punctually at the institute. She was met by a friendly, somewhat pompous man, Mr. Silverman, who seemed preoccupied with his managerial tasks—firing instructions and asking questions on his walkie-talkie while rushing through endless hallways and huge rooms, pointing on the way, absentmindedly, to installations and equipment. Carried away by his monologue, Mr. Silverman seemed to have forgotten about Olga. At one point on the tour, another man appeared from somewhere and suggested that she be taken to personnel to fill out some papers and meet the director of the institute. He was waved away and the meandering marathon continued. Out of breath, Olga was brought back from an almost dream-like state to reality by the words:

"What an attractive necklace," Mr. Silverman asked, his gaze fixed on Olga's neck. "Is it from Mexico? My wife and I came back from Acapulco a couple of weeks ago. My wife bought some jewelry there."

Taken aback, Olga tried to get back on track.

"No, it is not from Mexico," she said. "Could we discuss the position? Would you like to know something about my experience as a project engineer?"

"No need," he replied. "I have all the necessary information, as I told you on the phone. Everything is okay"

Confused and flushed with exhaustion, Olga did not press the point anymore.

An hour later, she was taken to the entrance door, told to wait for a phone call, and sent on her way. A week later, she called and was informed that the position had been filled. Incensed, she wrote a letter to the executive director, not quite clear what to expect but hoping for an explanation. There must have been a misunderstanding, she thought.

Three weeks later, she received a letter:

*Dear Mrs. Tomov,*

*I have received your letter of May 17th concerning your interview for the position of Chief Engineer with the Institute of . . . I am extremely sorry that the interview procedure caused you concern and appeared unfair. It is, however, a procedure which we feel from experience is suitable for this particular field. We believe it necessary to acquaint the applicant with the job's functions and requirements. Though it is a time-consuming process, we feel it is beneficial to the applicant and to the employer.*

*Finally, may I say that as with any hiring procedure, our concern was to employ the individual most suitable for our needs. It is true that the experience was not a prerequisite. I am sorry that the long interview procedure was a strain. The same interview procedure was used for all candidates because it is our belief that a short interview is unfair both to the applicant and to the employer.*

*Yours truly,*
*P.D. Shultz, Ph.D.,*
*Executive Director*

Olga was immensely flattered to learn that she had been interviewed for the position of chief engineer. She was also surprised that she was only one of many applicants, and even that she was interviewed. Indeed, the letter was sensible and only a poor loser or an overreacting wimp would have questioned the procedure, she thought. Yet Olga did not feel like any of the above and was determined to find out who the successful candidate was.

It turned out that a retired technician was hired. Evidently, very little in terms of education and experience was required for the position of chief engineer. At first, Olga had felt uncomfortable with the possibility that she was considered only because she was a female, but now she saw that she had nothing to worry about. In the end, it did not mean a thing.

Shortly after the ill-fated experience, still smarting with resentment and certain that she had been used—and vowing never to let it happen again—Olga was ready to confront her boss, Greg Baker. A couple of years had elapsed since her last raise. She thought that it was long overdue and that she deserved it.

"A raise?" he said. When was your last one?"

"Almost two years ago," she replied.

Greg looked surprised.

"Why didn't you ask me sooner?" he said. "I had forgotten. Sure, you deserve a raise. I will call Mary immediately."

Mary was in charge of accounting and personnel.

The "good news" infuriated her even further—it seemed that everything was her fault.

Olga was ready for a change, and from experience she knew her best chance was working through the agencies.

◆          ◆          ◆

## All about restless designers and exotic food

One of the places she was sent to was Universal Machinery Co. The position was a design draftsman, which was a notch up from her present designation.

The first thing she was asked to do was to take a test. It was a few pages long and read like no other test she had ever taken, filled with multiple choice and true-false answers. It was all so confusingly simplistic that it made her wonder.

"Those must be tricky questions," she thought. Baffled, Olga agonized over each question, often selecting the opposite to the obvious answer. After she finished, the test was graded immediately, and she was told that it was a complete failure. She was close to tears.

"Would you please show me some of the right answers?" Olga pleaded.

The woman who administered the test pointed out a few mistakes. There had been no tricks.

*Just a stupid test*, Olga thought.

"But, madam, are those questions suitable for screening engineers?" she asked.

"They are misleading with their simplicity. It is almost insulting."

"I only administer the test, I don't make it up," the woman replied.

The woman had introduced herself as Helen. Olga felt that there was a hint of genuine sympathy in her voice.


A few weeks later, Olga received a call from another agency, again in regard to a position of a design draftsman. An interview was scheduled.

Once inside the building, she felt a sense of familiarity, which turned to certainty the moment she was handed a written test, which was to be completed before the actual interview. Immediately she realized it was the same test she had failed a few weeks earlier; furthermore, it was the same company!

Olga was out of the examination room in a matter of minutes. An interview with the head of the engineering department followed. A few days later she was contacted by the agency and told that the job was hers. The new company was in the business of design and manufacturing of packaging machines. There were twenty or so designers working there, and Olga was the only female.

The engineering office was a spacious room with a high ceiling and windows all across one of the walls, crowded by the large drafting boards that were arranged in two rows. The designers seated behind them, hidden from view from front and back, were hard to spot. All but a couple were born outside Canada. Scottish,

Portuguese, Bangladeshi, Hungarian, Welsh, Armenian, English, and a few other nationals were easy to identify by their accents. Most of the time, the office was quiet. Seldom would someone leave his place, and when they did, it was usually to approach another designer with a question, to take a peek at his drawing, or to exchange a few words.

Every day, just before lunch, though, the noise level would increase. Food was always the main topic of conversation. Dishes from all continents were discussed and recipes were exchanged. At lunchtime, the mixture of exotic smells filled the air, exciting the taste buds of some, while chasing others out. On occasion, Omar, Miguel, Harout, and Olga would go out to the greasy spoon diner around the corner for a meal of sausages and cabbage, washed down with a glass of beer.

Then came the quiet of the early afternoon, often to be broken by an outburst of singing, coming from the spot where Lesley's board stood. Nobody minded. Lesley had a large repertoire of charming Welsh songs that he sang in a voice just as beautiful as the melodies.

Most of the designers had permanent positions, but there were some who worked on contract and led almost nomadic lives: moving from place to place, crisscrossing the border between Canada and the United States. One of them, Jim Hart, seemed to have a particularly hard time deciding where to settle, wandering not just throughout the continent but also over oceans. He had dragged his family thousands of miles: from England to Australia, then to Canada, then soon afterward to Tasmania, and back to England. Each move was supposed to be the final one, which meant selling everything and starting all over again. He was now on his way back to Tasmania.

His return to England had been a disaster. He was greatly disappointed with his native country and, in retrospect, Tasmania had been the best place he had ever lived. His wife and their two children also wanted to return to this paradise, which they loved even more after they had left it. Now, short of cash, they were traveling in stages, so Jim was planning to work at Universal Machinery Co. only long enough to make some money for the last leg of the trip to his final destination.

During the lunch hour, after consuming his sandwich and coffee alone, he would pull out of his briefcase a shiny, promotional booklet of a house construction company in Tasmania and start flipping through its glossy pages. Jim was in the process of selecting a new home for his family. In particular, he was looking for a bungalow—a unique type of local architecture worthy of high praise as the most comfortable one of them all. And since he had previously owned and sold a couple of them, he spoke on the matter with authority.

A designer with solid experience in the packaging industry was considered a specialist, and finding employment was not much of a challenge for someone with such credentials. The job, though, was demanding and stressful, especially when testing a new machine. During the test phase, it seemed that all that could go wrong, did. The bangs and clatters of fast-moving parts and the messy floor covered with labels—spewed incessantly by the magazines—created the impression of chaos. The palpable sense of tension and anxiety brought all on edge. The machines operated at such high speed that it was impossible to detect a malfunction with the naked eye; only through the use of cameras and after running the film at slow motion was it possible to determine what was going on and what went wrong. And then the blame game started—long before the problems were cleared up. The designers were the first to fall under suspicion.

After one particularly stressful day at work, Olga ended up in the hospital, hyperventilating. *Maybe it is time to move on*, she mused to herself.

A few months later, she pulled her resume and updated it once again.

> *July 1969-June 1973:*
> *Draftswoman, ABC Electronics Ltd.*
> *Duties:*
>
> *July 1973-present:*
> *Design Draftswoman, Universal Machinery Co.*
> *Duties:*

Again, the search began. By October she had an offer. Another step up her professional ladder: design engineer at one of the largest companies in the world, W.L. Co. Before she left Universal Machinery, she was handed a letter of recommendation.

*To Whom it May Concern:*

*Olga has proved to be an able and tenacious designer with a flair for accuracy and detail. She has become a key member of our design team, and we would be delighted to rehire her if she wished to return.*

*Yours truly,*
*Universal Machinery Co.*
*B.J. Giddings*
*Engineering manager*

Accordingly, she left in good spirits. She had learned a lot, had proven herself, and had forged long-lasting friendships.

◆          ◆          ◆

## Mr. Haas' insecurities and the end of what could have been, if only . . .

W.L. was a large company, a place where one could easily spend a lifetime building a career, moving up or laterally into different departments—engineering, sales, marketing, processing. The building itself was a sprawling, one-story structure. Inside it was bright and clean, the air permeated with the sweet aroma of various ingredients used in the production of candies. Olga was given an office among the row of offices, which faced the street. Pleased, she hung her shingle on the wall over her desk and settled down to work.

Once again, she was the only woman in the department and the first to hold an engineering position in the company. It made her feel special. However, it did not take her long to realize that she had a lot to learn in an environment where engineers were not doing much engineering; that success was measured by how high one moved up into management. As for engineering, the way she knew it, there weren't many challenges.

There was a company shop, subsidized cafeteria, and nice colleagues. What more could Olga ask for? So the years uneventfully rolled by. The performance reviews she received regularly were always good, stating that she was ready for a promotion as soon as a suitable position became available. Since there was no turnover of engineering staff, the promise did not mean much. Nevertheless, Olga was satisfied with the way things were.

It came as a surprise to her when the time for her review in the middle of the fifth year came and went without any mention of it. It was also the time when her immediate supervisor was to retire. She made some inquiries about the overdue evaluation of her performance, but instead of answers, received only elusive comments.

The day she was finally called in to the chief engineer's office to discuss the review, she found the atmosphere heavy with tension. Her outgoing supervisor, Mr. Vanderstein, was already there, seated next to an empty chair, presumably the one left for her. The chief engineer, Mr. Haas, was seated behind his large desk. His face was flushed, and he had a look of fanatical determination in his eyes. Mr. Haas was known to go through bouts of impulsive, strange behavior, but there were some additional signs that took Olga aback.

The room's décor was enhanced by a new item: a photo of the backside of a hippopotamus was prominently displayed. Its size, frame, and place on the wall were identical to the placement of the shingle that hung in her office. The prevailing opinion among her colleagues was that the chief engineer's lack of an engineering degree made him feel vulnerable and insecure in his position. Most figured this was the reason for his occasional overzealousness in carrying out his duties, which put him in proverbially comic situations. He was unpredictable, and that was worrisome.

Slowly and deliberately, Mr. Haas started to read the review. It stated that Mrs. Tomov's performance was marginal and a raise was not forthcoming.

She was shocked. The comments immediately struck her as preposterous, completely false, and unwarranted.

As she listened, her amazement grew, her heartbeat quickened, and she felt giddy. Next to her, Mr. Vanderstein sat on the edge of his seat, his head hanging down, his eyes hidden behind lowered lids. It was becoming suffocatingly hot in the office as the words just bounced off Olga's head. She could no longer hear anything.

The chief engineer finished reading and pushed a piece of paper across the table.

"Olga, sign this," he said.

"Are you kidding? "Olga heard herself shout." Do you really think that I will sign this nonsense? This is crazy!"

She jumped from her seat, brushing against Mr. Vanderstein, and stormed out of the office. A couple of minutes later she was in her overcoat, leaving her office almost in a run and heading toward the side exit of the building.

She got home in the early afternoon—angry, humiliated, and sick. All her frustrations and disappointments culminated in this moment. She could not contain herself anymore; she had reached the point of no return. She would scream and scratch and tell the whole world how she felt.

For now, she decided to write a letter to Mr. William White, the president of the company.

Very early the next morning, after a sleepless night of writing and rewriting a letter of complaint, she waited outside the president's empty office. She did not have an appointment, and did not even think about phoning beforehand, so she was not expected. But as soon as the secretary saw her, she realized that it would be impossible to send away this determined woman who wouldn't take no for an answer. Immediately after Mr. White arrived, Olga was ushered into his office.

Mr. White was very surprised at Olga's story. He listened attentively without interrupting even once. He let her pour it all out. Then he took the letter she handed him.

"Mrs. Tomov, I have to make some inquiries before I comment on your situation, but I commend you on your courage to bring the matter to my attention," Mr. White said. "Thank you. I will be in touch."

Olga went back to work both relieved and depleted. She knew that no matter what Mr. White said or proposed to do, she would not remain at W.L. for much longer. She now hated the place, hated her job, and she hated the chief engineer with his vulgar picture on the wall. The time had come once again to update her resume.

*June 1973-October 1974:*
*Design Draftswoman, Universal Machinery Co.*
*Duties:*

*October 1974-present:*
*Design Engineer, W. L. Co.*
*Duties:*

It was the end of the school year, and colleges were advertising for faculties for the following academic term. Mrs. Tomov applied and was called for an interview. The interview went well and she received an offer. It was as simple as that. A cut in salary and no security for further employment beyond one school year were small drawbacks. She was eager to leave W.L. and ready for a fresh start. She could not even wait until August—the starting time for her new job. She served notice on the company and, in the middle of June, picked her separation papers and left.

Some time before that, she received a letter from Mr. White. He had learned of her decision to resign from W.L. Co. and to pursue a career elsewhere. He expressed regret that she was leaving, thanked her for her contribution, and wished her every success in her new career. The same sentiments were echoed by the head of the personnel department.

This brought to an end Mrs. Tomov's career in engineering, or what she believed an engineering career ought to be. But before she immersed herself totally into teaching rather than doing, she received a call and a letter that lifted her spirits.

The call was from the former president of Universal Machinery Co. He had left his old employer and now headed a new company. He asked Olga to join. There was a particular project he had in mind for her: the development of a new packaging machine. She declined.

Three weeks into the semester, another letter arrived. It was from a human resources consultant company.

*Dear Mr. Tomov,*

*My firm is presently engaged in an extensive search for competent candidates for several management positions.*

*With your excellent qualifications and record of achievement, you may be interested in the unique career development potential offered by my clients. Within a metal fabrication, heavy manufacturing environment, the positions are:*

*Vice President Manufacturing*
*General Managers*
*Project Engineer*
*Superintendent of Manufacturing*
*Assistant to the Secretary Treasurer*
*Sales Managers*

*I look forward to your reply.*

*Yours truly,*
*(signature)*

What could have been, she thought, if only she had been a "mister."

◆          ◆          ◆

### Resigned, or the meaning of "happily ever after"

Finally, Mrs. Tomov had found her niche. She was happy. She felt that this was going to be a good ride. Once again she was the only female in her department, and all her students were male. With time, there were changes.

Some of her colleagues, though, never got used to her, and some of the students never did, either. Quite a few kept on calling her "sir." But there were plenty of others who made a difference.

It was not a surprise to her to be confronted on the first day of a new semester by a classroom-full of male students with stunned faces and nervous giggles. They had never imagined that a woman would be teaching them Strength of Materials or some other core subject. Some continued to challenge her throughout the semester; however, it was much easier for her to deal with provocation from the position of authority. So she came to enjoy the classroom experience, and found it most rewarding.

Besides the teaching, there was much more to the job. The ever-changing faces of students from all over the world reflected another worthy aspect of her new employment. All the stories they had to tell! Some were interested in her tale.

"Mrs. Tomov, where are you from?" they would ask. "Are you from . . . ?"

The years were rolling by fast. The resume was forgotten, for Mrs. Tomov never contemplated a change. Frustration, anger, weariness were things she always managed to get over, maybe because she never stopped believing that things could get better, "only if . . ."

Thus she continued to write letters to chairmen, deans, and vice-presidents in the quest for fairness and justice.

The world had changed considerably since she had graduated as an engineer: from slide-rulers and T-squares to drafting machines, calculators, and computers; from the structured, stiff, and strict to the flexible, casual, and inclusive.

The adjustment one had to make! The things one had to learn!

◆          ◆          ◆

It was the last—open book—test in the last class of Machine Design. Twenty-six students, crowded in a small and stuffy classroom, were fidgeting—crammed behind tables with hardly enough surface space to spread their books and notes on. Mrs. Tomov was distributing the test papers, squeezing between tight rows of chairs and tables along paths obstructed by bulky bags left on the floor and feet sticking out clad in a variety of over-sized shoes. Judging by the expressions on the students' faces, she concluded that the questions were not as easy as she had first thought them to be. Besides, she was a bit on edge.

A few moments earlier, she had noticed a number of students heading toward the very back of the room, taking seats packed close to each other—too close for her comfort. She had asked them to move voluntarily forward to the front. Nobody had responded to the invitation; she was kept waiting. Finally, Majdi had picked up his books and taken a place right in front of her table. She had resumed handing out papers, though, still smarting with annoyance with the incident.

The door opened and Saeed entered. He was late, and he was marching straight to the back.

"Don't go there. It is too crowded," Mrs. Tomov snapped while continuing her walk.

As she turned around to check the situation, she spotted Saeed sitting down at the very same table vacated by Majdi shortly before. Her reaction was swift.

"What are you doing? Didn't you hear what I said?" she asked.

Saeed was standing, his bag on the chair, flashing angry looks at her.

"Don't give me a hard time! What do you want?" he shot back in a loud, sharp voice.

She felt the blood draining from her face, anger swelling in her chest.

"Get out of the room!" she ordered, her voice rising to a high pitch.

He started to walk away.

"Pick up your bag, also," she added curtly.

He turn around, took his bag and left.

Silence descended on the room. It was startling. She stood, her feet rooted to the floor, clutching the bunch of leftover papers in her hands.

"Go on, go on," she muttered. "Nothing terrible has happened."

What Mrs. Tomov meant was for students to go on with their shuffling of papers, exchanging of whispers, behaving as usual. It had no effect. The deadly silence persisted.

After finishing the task of distributing the papers, Mrs. Tomov moved to the front of the classroom, and sat at her desk. A few minutes later, a slight tap on the door summoned her to get up from her seat and go to take a look. Outside, leaning against the opposite wall of the hallway stood Saeed.

"May I come in?" he asked

"Are you feeling all right?" she replied.

"Yes, I felt all right before," he snapped.

"Come in," she said, disregarding the implied challenge in his statement. "Pick up your test and bring it here," she continued while pointing to the place next to Majdi.

He did so calmly, and Mrs. Tomov assumed her position behind the front table, facing the entire class.

An oppressive silence still hung over the room mutated only by the persistent whirring of shuffling paper. A comforting thought crossed her mind: it was a test like any other, not better, not worse. She was back to earth. She felt confident and in command. It must have been her awareness of the moment, the significance she attributed to it, which made her feel sentimental and vulnerable for a while. Dressing for work earlier that morning in a pumped-up, almost euphoric mood, she had put on her best suit.

Suddenly the silence was broken: Amanda sneezed. In unison, a multitude of "Bless yous" rang out from the direction of twenty-six heads bowed over test papers. The tension dissipated; giggles followed. Yes, it was a test like any other. And clearly, it was an ordinary day in the everyday life of college.

"It is good to retire, after all!" she thought.

It was time to clear her office. Mrs. Tomov had been postponing this moment for as long as she could; there was too much stuff collected over the years. All of it had to be sorted out: some designated to the garbage can, and some, worth keeping, to be packed and taken home.

It required lots of time and effort to manage the task. The drawers were full of papers; their contents long forgotten. The cabinet was stacked with piles of old drawings, project reports, and books. The walls were covered with posters and pictures of students receiving awards or bunched in groups, posing behind projects they had completed: mechanical arms, wind tunnels, things like that. Next to them were thank you cards and obsolete calendars, many of which were attached to the wall by nothing stronger than scotch or masking tape with rough edges, put there on the spur of the moment. Now, they all looked precious. It was too hard to decide which ones to chuck out and which ones to keep.

Then there was the large poster of Albert Einstein that covered the wall behind her desk with the quotation: "Great spirits have always encountered violent opposition from mediocre minds." It was an arrogant statement to some, but a mantra to Mrs. Tomov. At some point, somebody had drawn a circle with a red marker around the great physicist's right eye. It made him look as though he was wearing a monocle; Mrs. Tomov thought that was rather cute.

Or how about the poster next to it, depicting a young girl sitting cross-legged, holding a pair of pliers in one hand, the other resting on a bicycle wheel with a text printed in bold, black letters stating, "I want to be an engineer just like my mom"?

Or the front cover of a program for the opera *Fidelio* by Beethoven, or the print of the painting *By the Seashore* by P.R. Renoir, not to mention the expired Chinese calendar with a pair of pigs—one black and one white?

With the passage of time, some had become wrinkled and some had faded. But all of them carried a poignant message that had helped Mrs. Tomov stay the course. For the moment, the task of sorting all these mementos of bygone times was overwhelming her. Eventually, she started pulling down everything, rolling it all up into bunches and placing it in bags to take home, thus postponing the decision.

Down came the two shingles: the certificates from the Associations of Professional Engineers of Alberta and Ontario, issued in January 1971 and January 1976, respectively. Promptly, they were placed into one of the bags stuffed with papers, then moved out of the room and left leaning against the outside wall of the office. Next, the desktop was cleared and the computer turned off. The sunrays penetrating through the venetian blinds covering the large window running all across one entire side of the room shone over the dust-covered computer screen and the bare white walls.

The last thing left to be done was to change the recorded message on the phone. Mrs. Tomov took her place behind the desk, lifted the receiver from the stand and, after a short pause to collect her thoughts, completed the required steps for recording an "extended absence" greeting. Then she began talking into the receiver with the most professional voice she could muster:

"Hello, this is Mrs. Olga Tomov. I will be away for an indefinite period of time. If you require assistance in my absence, you may dial zero and our department assistant will help you. Thank you."

"Indefinite period of time?" What a way to define her retirement! She simply could not do better. After hearing the message, to make sure it sounded all right, she replaced the receiver and glanced around the room one last time. A bright orange spot on the door of the cabinet drew her attention. It was a small sticker that read "Don't let the turkeys let you down," given to her a few years earlier by her daughter. With a smile she carefully peeled it from the gray, metal surface of the cabinet door and tucked it away in her wallet.

It was time to go. As she opened the door, she was surprised to see yet another, bigger yellow sticker attached on the outside.

> *Dear Mrs. Tomov,*
>      *We heard that you are retiring and came to your office to say "good-bye"*
> *and "thank you." We will try to see you before you leave.*
>      *We will miss you. Best wishes for your retirement!*
>
> *Alice and Jim*

Again, she carefully peeled the paper from the painted surface of the door and put it in her wallet, next to the turkey sticker. There was nothing more to do but lock the office door. Automatically, she shoved her hand into her deep, oversized handbag and fumbled through the variety of pocketbooks, change purses, and papers inside it in search of the ring with the numerous keys of different classrooms, offices, and labs. The feeling of frustration she had experienced every time she had gone through the same search, year upon year, came over her.

Suddenly she was struck by a thought: this empty, sterile-looking place was no longer hers. With a sense of relief, she quickly pulled her empty hand out of the overstuffed, bulging bag and muttered, "What the hell."

She turned around, picked up the bags packed with memorabilia, and proceeded to the parking lot.

A few days before her retirement, Olga came across her old, practically abandoned resume. She found it among a pile of old test papers, where it had remained hidden and unused for the past twenty-three years. She read it with mixed, conflicting feelings of detachment and sentimental affection. On an impulse, she grabbed a pen and scribbled under the last entry:

*August 1979-May 2002:*
*Professor, College of Applied Arts and Technology.*
*August 1992-August 1999:*
*Program Coordinator,*
*Duties:* ☺

Then she put it back in the top drawer of her desk.

In the empty room, stripped of all that once distinguished it as Mrs. Tomov's office, the only remainders of her were tucked away in the top drawer of the desk. There they were, hidden and forgotten, the final, and now complete resume, covered by a scattered bunch of business cards that read: "Olga Tomov, MESc, P. Eng."

# *The Forum*

Nevena Jones threw herself on the couch, flustered with agitation. She had just turned off the computer abruptly, wishing that she could shut off the whole world just as easily: with the flick of a switch.

For Ms. Nevena Jones, restless and weary, was coming to a crossroad, contemplating another change in her life—as always, "for the better". It seemed that she had let her enthusiasm carry her a bit too far.

◆         ◆         ◆

Another place, another time:

A half-empty classroom with only a few students inside, clustered together in front of the blackboard. All the students were dressed in uniforms—the girls in black frocks with white collars and either short or long braided hair; the boys in dark blue or black pants, white shirts, and short, bristled hair. The walls of the room ornate with rows of portraits of bearded and mustached men staring far into the distance with determination and boldness, presumably into a world that could be penetrated only by the gaze of immortals. The most prominent of these was a combined portrait of a most formidable duo: the dominating image of Karl Marx superimposed on the image of Frederick Engels—the latter's profile appearing like the shadow of his famous associate—its outlines somewhat distorted.

It was the long break in-between classes. Most of the students had gone out; some had sneaked into the washrooms to have a puff of a cigarette, while others had stepped down to the schoolyard to expend energy—enthusiastically kicking a soccer ball, or improvising fancy jumps shooting a ball through a hoop hanging from a wooden pole high above their heads. Meanwhile, the small group of students, mostly girls, that remained inside the classroom was engrossed in a lively discussion—nothing unusual for a bunch of feisty teenagers filled with social consciousness. Except that this was a lofty idea they were tackling on both sides of an unusual argument—an idea seldom put to a debate.

It was sparked by a shocking story that, in the last few days, had gripped the imagination of young and old alike. A crime had occurred. Of course, it was not reported in the newspapers or mentioned on the radio broadcasts. That simply was not done. But the rumors spread quickly. Whatever the facts, the verdict was not in dispute. Therefore, even though the discussion was provoked by an actual event, the arguments presented were about justice with regards to a hypothetical case.

The story went like this:

> *A university student had been stabbed in the back by a teenage boy while both were riding on a streetcar. Nobody was aware of the incident for a while; nobody had seen it happen. Strange as it may sound, it was possible. As usual, the car was packed with people, cramped and squeezed on all sides, and a great amount of pinching, stomping, and elbowing was going on. Nobody paid much attention to a groan, a squeal, or a curse.*
>
> *At a stop, the assailant had pushed his way through and disembarked. To the horror of the rest of the passengers, the victim had collapsed in the newly created open space. Pandemonium had ensued.*
>
> *Only a few hours later, a teenager was apprehended in his house in one of the city's suburbs—his parents left in dismay and shock. By then, the victim had succumbed to his wound. It was now murder! Soon, a detail emerged: the student was the president of the University Chapter of the Komsomol Organization. Nothing was known about the teen.*

Well, some had their suspicions . . .

Every day, new tidbits of small details were added to the story, feeding speculation and sparking discussion just like the one the students were involved in. At the onset of the rumor, there was a universal understanding and acceptance that the perpetrator of this awful crime would face execution. It was the right thing to do. Justice had little to do with fairness but much to do with unyielding vigilance and the righteousness of a society marching toward a perfect state for perfect people.

Back in the classroom, somebody had suggested that the new revelations about the circumstances of the crime had changed the perspective on the original story and brought some doubts regarding past judgments. Maybe it *hadn't* been the hooligan who had done it? (By now it had been accepted that the teen was a hooligan). Maybe there had been a motive?

Among all these excited, gesticulating, screaming participants stood a pretty, bright-eyed girl with her hair in a single thick braid that hung down below her waist. Her passion was supreme: each of her gestures was more expansive than anybody else's, and each of her statements was louder and more emphatic than anybody else's.

"There is something fishy about the whole story! There are not enough facts!" she repeated adamantly.

The rebuff that came from one of the other students was just as forceful.

"The fact is that a guy was killed and only a hooligan would do such a thing. And you are just a silly, naive goose!"

◆    ◆    ◆

This was Nevena's day off from work. She had spent the afternoon driving from one plaza to another, shopping in preparation for her trip back home—a place she had left over thirty years before, when the direction of her somewhat predestined future had taken a sharp turn after a faithful meeting with Colin Jones, a Canadian, on a visit to her native country. The relationship that had begun as a simple working arrangement between an interpreter, Nevena, assigned to accompany a tourist, Colin, on a sightseeing trip, had evolved into a personal and romantic affair. After spending a couple of weeks together, from morning till late evening, visiting the most charming places along the coast and enjoying lovely panoramas from majestic mountain tops, they had fallen in love. It must have been destiny! Eventually, they got married, and after a prolonged and cumbersome process, she was allowed to return with Colin to his country.

Once there, though, things did not work out the way either of them had expected. It was a clash of cultures or irreconcilable differences, or both. After a few years, there were still no children to bond them together and by then, she had become self-sufficient and no longer had to rely on her husband for support. With a good knowledge of English and a recognized degree in biology, she had found a job in a large pharmaceutical company and felt reasonably independent financially. Eventually, they divorced. Nevena chose to keep the Jones name.

Time had slipped by fast. Nevena was now in her fifties, and was feeling increasingly lonely and anxious. Meanwhile, she had experienced a few inconsequential relationships, all of which had left her with more bad memories than good ones, never able to find the warmth and understanding she craved.

The past couple of years, she spent her summer vacations in the old country. She was surprised to discover how much better she felt there, surrounded by warm and friendly people who struck her as passionate and exuberant—something she must have forgotten or merely failed to appreciate over the thirty previous years. She did not feel lonely there, indeed.

Maybe she could retire and move there? The advantages were ample, both financially and emotionally. With her pension she would be able to live far better there. With her savings she would be able to buy a nice place anywhere in the country while the best she would be able to manage here would be to retain her small condominium. There, she would be able to travel all over Europe—an attractive dividend—for, in her heart, she felt that she had never really left the old continent. To top it all off, the country was blessed with beautiful scenery: a wonderful seashore and lovely mountains. And the climate? There was no comparison with her present homeland. The possibility of returning permanently was slowly turning into a viable option to be considered. A month earlier, Nevena had made up her mind. As a matter of fact, she was planning to start looking for a property by the sea on her upcoming vacation.

Ever since her first trip there, Nevena had been trying to reconnect with the people of her native country. The Internet was an easy way to bridge the gap of thousands of kilometers. Every day she would read the online editions of several newspapers, visit sites providing information, services, and advertisements of all sorts, getting the feel of how things were there now. She diligently followed all new developments, advancements, and tragedies reported. The forthcoming entry into NATO, the anticipated integration with the European Union, all were contested and difficult propositions that, as far as she was concerned, were steps forward, for those changes would transform the place and make it easier for her to readjust. Oh yes, she had her doubts. It was hard to ignore the sense of relief she inadvertently experienced each time she returned from her vacations. She liked to think that it was merely the lack of conveniences that she missed over there and that this would be remedied once the country moved into a new direction.

One day, a couple of months earlier, while reading the English edition of the news, on an impulse, she clicked on the forum. Fascinated, she could not stop scrolling down the computer screen, reading page after page of comments posted by a seemingly countless number of people with all kinds of screen names—some hilarious, others outright cocky. Also, there was a bit of international flavor to the forum.

Hesitantly at first, she posted an opinion. The next day, she added another comment, then another opinion. Soon she became emboldened enough to start posting entire paragraphs—dispensing wisdom, entering into discussions of current events, matching wits with what she thought to be predominantly younger people. It was exciting being faceless, immune from being discarded because of age or looks, or whatever. Enthusiastically, she went on "reintegrating" herself with this younger generation that she had not witnessed growing up, while becoming more confident that there was indeed a lot of common ground and she would fit in.

On one of her ever-so-pleasant respites in front of the computer, engaged in what was by now her favorite pastime—chatting on the forum—her attention was drawn to one of the least controversial news items. It was an announcement that a politician had been killed in a car accident. He had been speeding along a road in bad weather conditions. His car had hit black ice, and he had lost control of his vehicle, crashing into the oncoming traffic. His death was instantaneous; nobody else had been hurt. This had been the information given regarding the circumstances of the mishap. A flood of opinions and comments were posted. Too numerous and, frankly, too passionate for that type of news, Nevena thought. Unanimously, all expressed the same sentiment: the man deserved to die.

Something stirred inside Nevena. Before she knew it, there was her opinion; the last one posted: "You people must be sick. A man deserves to die because he was speeding? How many deserve to live then?"

Upset and unsettled, she turned off the computer and didn't return to the site for a couple of days.

No matter how hard she tried to put it out of her mind, the story kept popping up into her thoughts, evoking recollections of her vacations there. She thought about how she was almost wiped off the sidewalk by a speeding car that had climbed over the curb; she recalled drivers honking at cars in annoyance at them obeying the yield sign for pedestrians.

Nevena was beginning to reconsider her online outburst. Maybe she had been too harsh and unreasonable.

She finally logged on and revisited the site. The column with comments had grown to twice as many opinions. It seemed that everybody had something to say, and it was all in response to her post.

"You idiot ! Because of people like you, innocent die," someone called Sweetflower had replied.

"You are the sick one! To think that speeding is an innocent crime!" was what Spartacus had written.

Nevena read them all. After a short contemplation, she put something together.

> *I am glad to have sparked this vehement discussion—it turned out to be quite enlightening. The anger expressed by most of you has nothing to do with this story, does it?*
>
> *I said what I said based on the facts given. It seems that many of you knew this man personally and are well aware of his character and general disrespect for human life.*
>
> *I did not. I assumed that he did not start his journey with the intent to kill anybody or himself. I am even inclined to give him the benefit of the doubt that he was in a hurry to see his sick wife.*
>
> *My condolences to his family.*

Once done, she clicked on the send button and quickly flicked off the computer.

It took Nevena quite a long time to collect herself as she lay on the couch listening to her pounding heart. In due time, she felt calm enough to get up and walk to the window of her apartment overlooking a quiet, narrow street with a park at the opposite side. It was a pretty picture: well-maintained grass, plenty of trees, and colorful patches of flowers arranged in neat patterns. In the children's playground farther away from the road, a couple of toddlers were playing, watched over by a young woman standing close by.

For a while, Nevena just stood there, her eyes following the golden glow of the sun slowly disappearing behind a cloud. Then she turned away from the window and headed straight for the kitchen. She was getting hungry. On the way, she glanced at a pile of boxes and shopping bags full of stuff ready to be put in a suitcase. A few steps later, as she passed the console standing along the wall, she caught a glimpse of a portrait of a young, bright-eyed girl with a single braid of hair hanging below her waist. She halted for a moment, gazing at the image.

"You silly goose!" Nevena muttered.

# The Letters

*To those from the class of 1955, scattered over four continents by the cold winds of an invisible war, once fought between two worlds divided by an impenetrable curtain.*

Vera shifted her gaze from the blank sheet of paper in front of her to the sunlit panorama outside the windowpane. She had been staring at the empty page of a fancy letter confectionery for quite a while, lost in a tangled web of thoughts.

It was most unusual for her. Ordinarily, filling page after page with smooth, well-organized sentences that flowed effortlessly from the tip of her pen was anything but a challenge. This letter, though, was special—very far from an ordinary one. It was to convey some extraordinary news to her parents, tidings they all had been hoping for for a long time. It had to be perfect!

Vera glanced at the magnificent mountains that surrounded the city. The rolling hills were covered in vegetation, scorched by heat and interspersed with splashes of tree groves spiked by elegant palms. It worked. Her muddled thoughts cleared. She was going to keep it short and simple.

> *Dear Mom and Dad,*
>
> *Sorry for the delay. I had to be absolutely sure before telling you the great news. We are going to have a baby! The due date is the eleventh of March, less than five months from now!*
>
> *I am feeling fine and plan to work till the end of the year. We haven't made any plans yet regarding my return to work after the birth of the baby. However, we are planning to go to the coast one of these weekends, or maybe even to Tacarigua for a few days.*
>
> *I am thinking of you a lot, now more than ever, wishing you could be with us in this happy time—and especially when your first grandchild arrives.*

*I am ending the letter; there isn't much else to write about. All my thoughts are about the baby and you. Special greetings from Ivan.*
*Keep healthy!*

*Hugs and kisses,*
*Vera*

◆          ◆          ◆

A few months later, thousands of miles to the north, a woman in her early thirties scribbled quickly on a piece of lined paper. She was seated at a desk inside a small, windowless office illuminated by the stark light of a luminescent lamp mounted on the ceiling. Occasionally, she would interrupt her activity to take a bite from an egg salad sandwich followed by a sip of coffee from a Styrofoam cup.

It was her lunch break and she was writing a letter to her parents—much like her friend Vera. This, however, was just an ordinary letter, part of her correspondence routine that she had maintained for years. Diligently, twice a week, every Monday and Thursday, she would squeeze a few extra minutes from her busy schedule to put pen to paper and write a letter to her mother and father to keep them informed about all aspects of her life: from the mundane to the extraordinary. Just like her friend Vera.

*Dear Mom and Dad,*
*I am writing this letter during my lunch break, so it will be short. Nothing new at work; just milling along. The weather is cold and unpleasant; the days are so short. Hate to have to work from dark till dark.*
*Didn't do much during the weekend—Annie got sick again. It never fails; she always gets sick on Friday afternoon. We would pick her up from school and she would slumber on the backseat of the car. It scares me so. Her temperature shoots and we end up taking her to the hospital. This past Sunday we had to take her there again. The doctor in the emergency remembered us! They gave her some medication and her temperature dropped to normal. Still, we decided to keep her home for a while, so Michael took a day off work to be with her.*

*For Annie's birthday we are planning a small celebration at home, just the three of us, and on the weekend following it we will take a few of her friends to a movie and then to MacDonald's for hamburgers.*

*Otherwise, nothing new. Thank you for your last letter. Mom, please give our regards to everybody.*

*Also, would you tell me why you sold the suit we sent you? It was made of the finest English wool cloth that you like so much. I thought that it would suit you perfectly and keep you warm. Is it a question of money? Please let us know.*

*Take care of your health!*

*Many kisses from the three of us.*

*Yours,*
*Lena, Michael, and Annie*

A miserable January day was coming to its end as fast descending darkness over the city ushered another cheerless and dreary evening in. Mounds of old snow that had been pushed off the road and covered with crust of gray ice obstructed the movement of pedestrians scurrying along slippery sidewalks. A chilly west wind lashed at their faces and brought tears to their eyes.

Impatiently, Lena pulled the ends of the shawl wrapped around her neck to tighten its protective grip while brusquely walking toward the mailbox next to the bus stop. She clumsily opened the slot with hands covered in thick mittens and pushed the envelope through. Then she entered the glass shelter and joined a small group of people waiting for the bus.

"Hallo!" Lena shouted into the telephone mouthpiece after emerging from the kitchen in haste and abruptly lifting the receiver. "Hallo, who is it?" she inquired.

An unfamiliar voice inquired back,

"Is this the residence of family Simovs?"

"Yes, it is."

"Am I speaking to Lena?"

"Yes, this is Lena speaking,"

After a brief silence interrupted by a crack in the line, a different, cheerful, booming voice came on.

"Lena! This is Philip! How are you?"

"Philip! Where are you?" Lena asked, breathless.

"In Mexico. Do you want to see me?"

The mischief in his voice was disturbing and perplexing.

"What do you mean? How? Are you kidding?" She reiterated, "What do you mean?"

"I am going to officiate in Edmonton for the Pan American games. And if you promise not to tell anybody, I will buy a ticket with a stopover at Toronto and spend a day with you. How about that?"

"Oh, Philip! I can't believe it!"

She beamed a happy smile.

"Tell me, when are you coming?" she asked, and was suddenly struck by a thought. "But how will we recognize you?"

The last time she had seen her cousin Philip, he was a slender, gawky teenager with huge hands which he easily wrapped around the water polo ball in a firm grip—a small indication of his potential for the game that he had so successfully mastered later. Now, he was someone she knew only from her mother's letters—from hints and messages wrapped in ambiguity.

"Look for a Mexican-looking guy with a big mustache," his booming voice cracked with laughter.

Lena couldn't stop giggling. This did not sound at all like the shy, quiet boy she remembered.

The crowd in front of the arrival gate of Terminal 1 was small. The passengers from the last flight had dispersed and only a few were still standing on the sidewalk, looking expectantly in the direction of the oncoming traffic. Michael slowed the car to a crawl, while Lena kept scouring the faces of the few waiting men. It didn't take long to spot the tall, sunburned, mustached man with broad shoulders and spindly legs, clad in colorful sports jacket and faded jeans. As a matter of fact, it was hard to miss him. The car had hardly come to a stop when Lena flew out of the door and threw herself against the man she did not know in her memory, but instantly knew in her heart. As Philip wrapped his arms around her in an embrace, she found her face buried in his chest, almost suffocating in the soft material of his jacket.

Back at the house, the first thing Philip did was to hand Lena an envelope addressed to Fam. Simovs.

"Here is a letter from your mom," he said.

The first thought that crossed Lena's mind was, *It is uncensored!*

Then, suppressing her urge to rip the envelope open immediately, she left it on the nearby table and turned toward Philip.

"Thanks! Now, tell us all about you and everybody."

It was a long evening spent reconnecting with conversation and reminiscences that brought back some of the closeness of old times. And when everybody had gone to bed, in the early hours of the new day, exhausted and excited, Lena opened the letter and began reading it under the pale light of a night lamp.

> *"My darling children, Lena and Michael, my golden Annie,*
>
> *Last Thursday we celebrated Annie's birthday. I made banitsa, Dad bought a bottle of red wine, the one we call velvet—remember, Lena? Also placed on the tables and the buffet small bouquets of spring flowers to brighten the place. All of our friends came: Mrs. Petrova, Mrs. Tsenova, Nina, Fanny, etc. All brought flowers and Nina even brought a box of Swiss chocolates from the Korecom. We talked and laughed and looked at your pictures. Everybody said you look wonderful, and that they enjoyed themselves at the party, and all send you greetings and best wishes; especially to Annie!*
>
> *Thinking of you! We love you! Many hugs and kisses to the three of you, to our precious Annie!*
>
> *Yours,*
> *Baba Anna and Dedo Liubomir.*

The first page of the letter ended there. There was more on the back.

> *P.S. My Dearest,*
>
> *Lena, you are asking why I sold the suit you sent me. First of all, it was red. You know how much your Dad hates this color! Besides, I don't feel like wearing bright clothes, there is nothing bright around me; we live in a gray and shabby world that is getting worse. The only joyful feelings we can experience are from the God-sent sunshine, and the only strength for living we derive is from your letters and your pictures.*
>
> *And we don't want you to send us money anymore. They don't give us dollars, and the bank gives us only a fraction of what they are worth. The*

*money from the suit will help us for awhile. We know how hard you are working; I only wish that I could have come to help you take care of Annie. To see her and Michael for the first time, to see you again. It breaks my heart when I read about Annie's illnesses, about your difficulties in raising a child alone, while we do nothing here, useless and vanquished. We are keeping our hopes up, though, as long as we are alive. And that makes it even harder to give you this very sad news: Vera's mother has passed away.*

*I learned about it accidentally when I came across a posted obituary bearing her picture. It was a great surprise for me, since I saw her not long ago and she was looking quite well. We did not have time for a chat. She had stopped just for a moment to tell me that she was on her way to submit an application for a passport and exit visa. Couldn't figure out why she is applying so soon after they refused her only six months ago. What a tragedy!*

*Vera must feel terrible! Add my condolences when you send her yours.*

*Your mom, Anna*

Lena folded the letter and put it back on the small table, next to the dry flower and the leaf of sweet geranium she had found inside the envelope. It was supposed to bring health.

The next day, Philip left. A few days later she sent Vera her and her mother's condolences.

The inevitable March storm came and went, wreaking havoc on the city, clogging streets and highways with thick cover of wet and heavy snow, exasperating everybody, from the drivers to the pedestrians navigating through slush and ice. But finally, the sunshine and the longer days prevailed—spring was in the air. The drudgery of winter was yielding to the jubilation of renewal.

A couple of months had passed since the day Lena received the letter bearing the news of Vera's mother. Immersed in big and small problems, coping with the challenges of everyday life, the regularity of correspondence between the two friends had never been high in the order of their priorities. So the lack of news from Vera did not disturb her. Besides, under the circumstances, it was natural—she probably needed to be left alone.

It was Lena's and Michael's wedding anniversary, and Lena had taken half a day off from work in order to get ready for the special dinner she had planned for the three of them. On her way in the house she had picked up the mail delivered earlier and quickly had checked the pile for a letter from her parents. There was none. So she put the pile away and got busy with her work. When everything was done—the table in the dining room set, the food ready and stored away till it was time to be served, the half-burned candles stuck in the silver candelabras replaced with new ones—Lena picked up the pack of mail again and started sorting it. Among the bills and junk mail there was a pale blue airmail envelope. The stamp was French and the return address was familiar. A happy smile brightened Lena's face.

> *Dear Lena,*
>
> *Thank you for your Christmas card and all good wishes! Did not write you sooner, was very busy after the holidays—lots of work had piled up at my job while I was away. Spent New Years in Essen with Mimi's family.*

For a moment, Lena stopped reading while trying to recall who Mimi was. Then she remembered. Mimi was a girl who attended the same school that she had attended and used to live close to Vera. Lena resumed her reading.

> *Mimi called on Christmas Eve and asked if we would go to visit them. She was organizing a New Years party and already had been in touch with Vesko and Lillie, Emil, and Nadia. All were going, so we decided to join. On the thirtieth of December the four of us jumped in the car and drove nonstop to Essen.*
>
> *The party was great! We stuffed ourselves with food, sang and danced till the morning. The following day headed back home.*
>
> *How did you spend the Holidays? Do you have any news? Have you heard from Vera?*
>
> *Last week got a phone call from Mimi to tell me that Vera had a baby boy. This is the good news. But an awful thing happened; her mother, Mrs. Minkova, passed away a few months ago. Mr. Minkov decided to keep it a secret from Vera for a while, till the baby's arrival. You know how long it took her to get pregnant; he did not want to upset her. Lo and behold, somebody sent her a card of condolences! What a shock! She did not lose the baby, but she got sick and is on medication.*
>
> *I am wondering if I should write to her?*
>
> *That will be all for now.*

*All the best to you, Michael, and Annie!*

*With love,*
*Dora*

*P.S. What are your plans for the summer? Any chance you might be coming to Europe? We would be very pleased to have you visit us!*

An hour later, a bang of the front door and a cheerful call announced Michael's arrival.

"Anybody home?"

Upstairs, Lena lay on her bed, pale and listless, with tears trickling down the temples of her face and sinking into the soft pillow leaving wet spots. Anguish had cast its shadow over her, and nothing would chase it away. The thud of Michael's feet running up the stairs did not break its spell, nor did his appearance by the side of the bed with a worried look in his eyes and a bouquet of red roses in his hand.

"What is the matter? Where is Annie?" Michael inquired, anxious and perplexed.

"Annie? Oh, Annie . . . she is all right. She's at the neighbors."

The words trailed into a halting, hardly audible whisper. In a feeble gesture, she raised her arm to Michael, handing him the pale blue envelope squeezed in the palm of her hand.

"Here, read this," she muttered through dry lips.

Michael complied.

After a short, contemplative silence, in a soft voice and carefully measuring his words, he ventured, "It is not your fault. You did not know. Your intentions were good," all the while bending over and stroking her arm soothingly.

"You rest. I will go and pick up Annie," he added meekly, then he turned around and left the room—the flowers still in the grip of his hand.

The muffled sound of the outside door slamming against the wood frame was shortly followed by a loud bang accompanied by Annie's excited twitter and Michael's subdued utterances.

It was time to pull herself together. A fleeting thought crossed Lena's mind: *"Have to write to Vera . . . soon."*

Reluctantly, she raised herself from the bed, wiped the tears from her eyes and cheeks, and headed toward the staircase. As she reached the edge of the top step and placed her hand on the baluster, she halted in hesitation for a moment, weak with fatigue. Suddenly, it dawned on her: *Tomorrow . . . tomorrow is Thursday!*

Buoyed by a sudden surge of energy, Lena quickly descended along the stairway, brushing away all thoughts off her mind, but one.

*Tomorrow, I'll write to mother. I'll write all about it to mother. I'll explain it all to her . . .* The load on her shoulders had eased; the anxiety had abated.

The first line of a letter rang through her mind:

*Dear Mom and Dad . . .*

# The Small Vendetta

This unique Canadian practice of multiculturalism that many of us feel so proud of is a good thing—I think. It is supposed to help us build a new, tolerant society in which people accept each other the way they are, and thus helps us create a more harmonious environment in a country where much of the population growth is due to the influx of immigrants.

Right?

However, in order for this policy to work, there are a few requirements of all of us, mainly that we should make an effort to acquaint ourselves better with other cultures. Otherwise, there could be great disappointments and even more dire consequences, which, then, we should not be blaming anybody for but ourselves for not doing our homework before getting into this painful predicament.

A story to illustrate my point:

Mr. and Mrs. Robert Jordan (abbreviation from Jordanoff—Mr. Jordan's ancestral family name a couple of generations back—the name his forefathers carried with them on a ship they had boarded somewhere in Europe and that had taken them to the port of Halifax) had neighbors, Mr. and Mrs. Luis Bertrand, who had a cousin, Mr. Castelletti, who lived in Corsica.

Mr. and Mrs. Bertrand were French—true ones, from France. Luis Bertrand was the representative of a French firm that owned the condominium next to Mr. and Mrs. Jordan's unit, situated in a prime location in a large Canadian city by a lake. For the last five years, the Europeans had called this two-bedroom apartment home. As it happened, the two families met early on, and hit it off right from the beginning—so well, in fact, that during a dinner party at Christmas time—their last one in Canada—they decided to spend their respective summer holidays together, touring the United States. Since Mr. and Mrs. Bertrand were due to return to France at the end of the following August of the coming year, this trip was regarded as possibly their last opportunity to go see some places they had been planning and wanting to see for the last five years, but had never had the chance to do so. Too much work, too little time. While it was to be a sightseeing trip for the Bertrands, for Mr. and Mrs. Jordan—who had already seen much of the land south of the border—it was to be a journey purely for the pleasure of the company and not to be underestimated, prompted by their willingness to serve as tour guides for their French friends.

It all seemed very convenient and fun.

The next few months passed by quickly, and preparations for the trip were falling into place: the schedule, the itinerary, and the routes were all discussed in length and agreed upon. The collection of maps and information pertaining to specific places of interest followed. Mr. and Mrs. Jordan brushed up on their knowledge of the geography and history of the few battlefields, national parks, and entertainment spots they were planning to visit. All was going very smoothly indeed, until a few weeks before the appointed date of the start of the trip; a small problem arose from an unexpected source—Mrs. Bertrand's cousin from Corsica, Mr. Antonio Castelletti, had decided to come and visit for a couple of weeks.

The replacement for Mr. Bertrand was scheduled to arrive before Mr. and Mrs. Bertrand were to take their flight back home upon their return from vacation, and that meant some overlap for the occupancy of the condo. Mr. and Mrs. Jordan graciously extended an invitation for the couple to spend a few days at their place at the end of the trip and before their departure, along with Mr. Castelletti, who had decided to join them on their journey. All seemed to work just fine.

The trip started on a perfect day; for what could be more important than the weather as far as vacations are concerned? And the day this one began on was nothing short of spectacular: the sun was shining from a pale blue sky through air so clean and translucent that it made the world sparkle as though seen through a freshly washed glass, all the way to the end of the horizon. It was a most wonderful start to a great journey to come, sure to be filled with adventure and enjoyment. At least this was how it felt to all.

The first stop for a brief rest was a couple of hundred kilometers down a newly widened highway, at a clearing of a section still bearing the signs of recent roadwork activities: the visible presence of a few huge, brightly colored construction machinery, a bunch of bright red pylons pushed to the edge of the concrete surface—ready for the finishing layer of asphalt—a few heaps of gravel here and there. It was a convenient place to stretch their legs, to munch on still-fresh sandwiches (with goat cheese and cucumber or egg salad), to take a few photos, and even to explore a bit of the surrounding nature.

The first overnight stop was at a motel that took a bit of time to reach a consensus about. It was a hard choice—unexpected but understandable, considering the expectations of five people all bent on expressing their preferences and demands. As a matter of fact, for Mr. and Mrs. Jordan—who were already feeling burdened by the sense of responsibilities as hosts trying to impress the foreigners with their wonderful country—anywhere would have been good enough. While Mr. and Mrs. Jordan opted for an early night and a snack consisting of a couple of sandwiches gone soggy from day-long exposure to the relentless sun penetrating the bags piled at the back of the rented SUV, Mr. and Mrs. Bertrand, along with cousin Castelletti, felt invigorated and ready for some exploration of the neighborhood, followed by a relaxed sit-down dinner—as only true Frenchmen could appreciate.

So, the group split up. In retrospect, this was the first sign of cracks that had started to creep into the veneer of harmonious coexistence that bound the group.

After devouring their dinner standing by the rented SUV, which was already parked for the night in the parking lot behind the motel, Mr. and Mrs. Jordan retreated to their room for the night while the others disappeared into the falling dusk. The next morning, all looking refreshed and ready for a new day of discovery and surprises, they boarded the dusty SUV and let a sigh of satisfaction at the sound of the engine ignition and the sensation of a smooth ride that followed.

And then, there was the border. It was not an experience any of the concerned wanted to remember. The funny thing was that it turned out to be less stressful for the French and the Corsican than it did for the neighborly Jordans. However, this has nothing to do with the point of the story rather than with the state of affairs in a world seemingly turning more complicated and confusing with each passing day.

The journey continued south of the border along a beautiful scenic route that curved through picturesque resort towns and peaceful lakes on both sides of the road. Meanwhile, inside the crowded SUV, a precariously grim situation was developing. It was coming from cousin Castelletti's direction, and it seemed to be fermenting from his frustration with his limited ability to communicate . . . perhaps a language problem? Alienated, sulky, and withdrawn, he refused to share in the driving, silently staring through the side window at the fast-moving countryside. Not a happy trouper by any account.

At the end of a ten-hour drive, everyone appeared to be ready for another overnight stop at a motel near a restaurant situated in a picturesque area with a great panoramic view. Dinner fell on one of the busiest times of the day and the service was slow. The situation was further aggravated by the sticky heat that drifted in from the outside and an air-conditioning system that rendered only a few comfortable spots right under the vents blowing cold air from the ceiling, creating a few oasis of relief for a spell. The cousin started fidgeting and requesting to be moved to a different table, away from the draft of hot air coming from the outside, as well as from the stream of cold air shooting from the ceiling—clearly, a difficult request to fulfill.

Throughout the ensuing commotion, he kept on speaking to the waitress in French while pointing to the food, the fan, the service, and even the funny-tasting water. With great discomfort, Mr. and Mrs. Jordan kept interpreting—struggling with their limited command of the French language—while darting harsh looks in Castelletti's direction, alternating with apologetic ones at the waitress till, finally exasperated, they abandoned all efforts to mitigate the situation and shut up. At this point, Mr. and Mrs. Bertrand tried to take the matter into their hands, but alas, to no avail.

In silence, all five headed straight to the motel perched on a hill and surrounded by lovely scenery.

The next morning began with a brief lecture delivered by Mrs. Bertrand to cousin Castelletti. It had an immediate effect: he got behind the wheel—on first sight a victory of a sort, but soon to be regretted. As soon as Mr. Castelletti wrapped his fingers around the driving wheel of the SUV and pressed his foot against the gas pedal, the SUV took off like a rocket and zoomed along the straight-as-an-arrow highway. Was this the revenge of a frustrated macho man, or just the normal driving habits of a European racing through the foreign countryside? One thing was for sure: what seemed as a remedy of a bad situation was proving to be a disastrous miscalculation.

Next day brought more of the same. The cousin was becoming more and more assertive. It appeared that, finally, he had found enjoyment. And as though trying to make up for lost opportunities, he took ownership of the driver's seat, refusing to yield it to anyone; driving faster and faster, watching with glee in his eyes as the needle quickly moved clockwise along the face of the speedometer. He beamed triumphant smirks at each successful overtake of a vehicle, which hastily receded in the far distance. He was giddy with excitement as girls threw astonished glares at him and the flying SUV packed with bobbing heads and shopping bags full of stuff.

At noon, there was a reprieve: a nonnegotiable break for a sit-down-midday-full-course meal—despite Mr. and Mrs. Jordan's persistent calls for a brief rest, quick snack, and a change of driver. Majority won, and an hour was spent in concentrated efforts of dealing with appetizers, main courses, and deserts. To the horror of Mr. and Mrs. Jordan, Mr. Luis Bertrand inquired about the wine list! Fortunately, alcohol was not served, and the party left behind just an empty jug of orange juice, as well as the comfort of the restaurant, and again squeezed one by one into their, by now, customary seats.

Four days into the trip, Mrs. Jordan began keeping a travel diary.

On the fifth day, the "happy gang," as they chose to call themselves at the beginning of their journey—and by now, an ironic, unsuitable designation—reached the city of B. The weather was beautiful and comfortably warm. It was midday and time for a lunch break. On the approach to their destination along an elevated stretch of the highway, Mrs. Bertrand enthusiastically went on and on at the sight of a gilded dome rising above the city's skyline. Her heart was set on seeing the building close up. Before going on the sightseeing expedition, the not-too-slight problem of finding a parking spot had to be resolved. Meanwhile, Mrs. Jordan kept trying to make a point by repeatedly stating that there was nothing special about this particular place. It was just another Midwestern backwater town.

Well, it did not work. Part of the group went off in search of the golden dome, while the Jordans took off in the opposite direction supposedly in search of a drugstore, looking for medicine strong enough for Mrs. Jordan's persisting headache. That accomplished, the Jordans kept walking around aimlessly for a couple of hours until the agreed-upon time to meet at the parking lot, by the SUV. The others showed up on time, breathless, sweaty, and red in the face, big shopping bags swinging from their hands.

*"What are those people doing? They came all this way just to go shopping?"* The thought that crossed Mrs. Jordan' s mind was wicked, and she knew it. She felt guilty.

Surprisingly, the following day—the sixth day of the journey—turned out to be a most relaxing one including a stop at a national park that featured breathtaking nature and wonderful scenery. All seemed to be in an agreement that this was God's country. Everyone took pictures, stopped at a souvenir shop in the park, and bought a few great presents for friends and relatives back home. More great time at the dinner table too. The cousin was in a good mood and even tried to crack a joke in English while flirting with the waitress!

At the city of C—on the seventh day of the journey—was a scorching 50 degrees Celsius! The group found a motel a bit further off the tourist area. Mrs. Jordan felt exhausted and couldn't find the strength to drag herself downstairs to the restaurant. Her husband, Bob, did get a couple of hamburgers and drinks from the McDonald's across the street and brought them up to their room. The couple spent the evening lying in bed, watching TV, munching on french fries and drinking Sprite.

Though, a most significant, consequential occurrence transpired this same evening. It started around eight o'clock with a knock at the door. There they were, Mr. and Mrs. Bertrand, all dressed up and ready to go; asked for—rather, demanded—the keys to the SUV, wished a pleasant evening to the Jordans and strode away. Glancing trough the window, Mrs. Jordan spotted the cousin standing by the SUV in the parking lot, waiting.

Something snapped inside Mr. Jordan. He realized the entire experience was turning into a farce! He made up his mind that the next morning he was going to tell them that he and the Mrs. were heading back home.

The following morning, everyone met in front of the SUV. There was no mention of the previous night. Mr. Jordan informed them in a steady and firm tone that he and Mrs. Jordan wanted to shorten the trip and start on the return journey. The news was met with silence and without great surprise. The cousin's face seemed to relax as well as harden at the same time while palpitating with intense feelings. A strange metamorphosis that was hard to describe.

On the way, there was a lot of laughter and conversation in French, presumably— Mrs. Jordan thought—all about last night. *Must have had a good time.* At the back seat of the SUV, the pile of shopping bags full of stuff had grown considerably.

The ninth day of the journey passed like a blur. Pushing hard forward, with a stopover at the city of D, where the group split two ways, as had become the usual practice: Mr. and Mrs. Jordan took off one way while Mr. and Mrs. Bertrand, plus cousin Castelletti, took off the other way. While meandering along the streets, the Jordans accidentally ran into the trio taking pictures of themselves in front of a monument. All waived at each other. Mrs. Jordan complained to her husband that she was feeling sickly and miserable.

Late in the afternoon on the following day, the weather turned bad. Dark, low floating clouds drifted in quickly from a dark gray horizon transformed into gauze, obliterating the divide between sky and earth. The rain came down suddenly in a gush, beating against the roof of the SUV in sheets driven by strong winds, pelting the windows mercilessly, and obscuring the view. It took close to an hour to locate a motel with vacancies in a small town off the highway, whose streets were filling fast with water. The place was enveloped in eerie darkness.

Exhausted, tired, and soaked, the now "unhappy gang" headed to dinner at a nearby restaurant. Mrs. Bertrand did not join them.

The entry in Mrs. Jordan's daily journal for the following day was brief and ponderous:

"Just driving . . . More tension . . . The scenery is lovely—must come back, alone with Bob, and enjoy . . . Next year, perhaps?"

She was overwhelmed with feelings of disappointment and regret.

On the day before the end of the journey, Mrs. Jordan grew more irritated by the hour. The entry in her travel log for the day read: "Drive, drive, drive . . . French, French, French . . ."

The last leg of the journey fell on the thirteenth day from its start.

"Crossed the border. Finally, it is over!" Mrs. Jordan wrote with relief in her journal.

So, it all came to an end—the highly anticipated trip, the fun, the expectations, and probably even the fast friendship between Mr. And Mrs. Jordan and Mr. and Mrs. Bertrand.

However, this remains to be determined in the future.

The slightly increased time left prior to the flight of the French—back home—the group spent under the same roof as prearranged. It was uneventful, and the parting was as cordial as possible in circumstances as strained as those, with the exceptions of Mrs. Bertrand's cousin Castelletti, from Corsica. While the Jordans and Bertrands went through the French ritual of kissing each other as many times as required by the customs of the French region Mr. and Mrs. Bertrand came from—all done in the spirit of reconciliation as well as of recognition of the culture of the guests—the cousin just stood away from the others, refusing to participate. His face was as gloomy as the overcast sky; his dark brown eyes narrowed to no more than two slits above his fleshy nose, and his head stuck forward in a posture that resembled the quivering body of a bull ready to attack.

Before the entire ritual came to an end, he was spoiling some of the amiable ambiance the others were trying so hard to maintain with a hiss under his breath directed at the hostess in a language she could not understand.

When all was over, Mrs. Jordan felt greatly relieved but emotionally drained to a point of physical illness. She went to bed early and slept soundly for the first time in the last couple of weeks. During the next few days, she felt sufficiently recuperated to start cleaning, washing, and in general putting the place in order. A couple of days elapsed before she got around to cleaning the guest room in which the cousin from Corsica had stayed. And when she did, she felt her heart sinking: a large water spot marked the outlines of a shaver on the top of a bookcase—one of a considerable sentimental value to her. The pieces of a broken decorative ceramic vase mingled with scattered dry flowers littered the floor. After a more thorough investigation, she discovered some more unsightly things in the bathroom that had been used by cousin Castelletti—all of which looked deliberate and conveyed a message to her that in her state of mind seemed quite shocking and without any doubt.

Not that all that mattered much, but Mrs. Jordan was very angry! However, her anger was not directed at the perpetrator of these little crimes, but toward herself. She should have known! Weren't Corsicans famous for their vindictiveness? After all, she was a Canadian, and as such she should have known indeed!

I think . . .

# *Enraged*

I am so angry! I can't get over it! So, I'll try to write it all down. Isn't that what the doctor prescribes? To get it out of your system?

The latest aggravation that is still turning my stomach inside out came about the following way:

This morning, after classes, I was sitting in the cafeteria having coffee all by myself and reading something I had just put down on paper: a recommendation for a student. I like the student; actually, he is one of my favorites, so I wanted to make a good job of it. Suddenly, from somewhere, I heard Paul Stevens' voice next to me.

"Hi, how are you doing?" he said. "No lunch? Hmm . . . I wonder if this sandwich is any good . . . Things are going from bad to worse around here."

I lifted my eyes from the letter to find Paul seated at my table opposite me, unwrapping a cheese and ham sandwich, carefully examining it, and all the while talking.

*What is his problem?* I think to myself. *Can't he see I am busy?*

Of course I don't say anything, just took a sip of my coffee and got back to reading my letter. But Paul does not get it. He kept going on.

"What are you reading?" he asked. "Some kind of memo? From the union? What do you think about the strike vote?"

For a while, I kept on reading without answering.

"No, nothing of the sort," I finally said. "I am writing a reference for a student. Actually, you know him: Roman Shapirovich. You must have taught him also. Drafting 101."

Suddenly, a thought crossed my mind.

"Do you mind reading it and maybe you could tell me if it is all right," I said. "I mean, if it is complementary enough, as well as truthful."

"Hmm," Paul said. "That will not be easy. This guy, what was his name . . . Shapirovich? Frankly, I think that he is a pompous ass."

With that, he took the piece of paper and began reading. Meanwhile, I was fuming on the inside. *What does he mean?* And just as I was ready to pull back the piece of paper, he leaned toward me and points out an expression.

"I would change this sentence," he said. "It does not sound right."

"What do you mean, 'it does not sound right?'" I asked. "Don't you understand the meaning?"

I proceeded to read the sentence, but he interrupted me.

"Yes, I do," he said. "What I mean is that in Canada we don't say that."

"Well, I am saying it, and I am in Canada."

Of course, I said all this with a smile and as pleasantly as I could, though I was angry as hell.

"I have been here for almost as long as you," I said with a chuckle.

By now, I was really laughing. And this is true—what I had just said. The guy was born here, but he is a young man who must have been a kid when I came to Canada. He is startled for awhile, but then he smiles at me, as he realizes that I am right. Or does he?

*"You don't get it! Do you?"* I think as I got up to leave him alone to munch on his sandwich of doubtful quality.

I rushed to the parking lot and jumped in my car. All the way home, I kept thinking about this. And now here I am, writing about it.

However, this is not the first time I have felt this way, and I am sure it will not be the last time. Maybe I should do something about it, like write down my previous experiences? Sort of cleanse myself.

So, let me tell another recent story that left me just as infuriated.

The other day, I happened to be visiting our next-door neighbors. Actually, it was an open house, and the place was full of people. It was a well-dressed, well-spoken crowd. No one had an accent—that is to say, no one besides myself.

Well, since I did not know anybody, I drifted from one small group to another, trying to participate in the conversations. It was not easy. Fortunately I noticed a couple of the guests standing by the staircase, each holding a glass of wine and looking up at the huge skylight on top of the open foyer, about fifteen feet up. I should mention here that this is the twin of our own house. As a matter of fact, we were the first ones that bought one of these houses—on paper—before it was built. There were only drawings on which I personally was involved. Some of the initiated changes were incorporated not only in our unit, but also in this one, as well as in the neighboring pair.

As I was moving toward the people standing by the staircase, I could hear them talking about the skylight.

"Isn't that a marvelous idea?" someone said. "I have never seen such a huge one."

"Hello," I said cheerfully as soon as I could interject myself into the conversation. "I am the next-door neighbor. This skylight was my idea. We requested that the builder put one in our house, and he decided to do the same for that one."

Since everyone in the group was looking at me rather startled, I thought I should explain further.

"You see, we bought the house first," I continued.

Finally there was a reaction.

"Good for you," said one of the ladies, who promptly turned her back to me to continue her chat with the others.

"I think, in this case it was rather good for Mr. and Mrs. MacTavish," I shot back.

A couple of people turned to look at me, puzzled.

"This is their home isn't it?" I added, looking at the faces now staring at me in silence.

I just turned around and moved away.

*"You don't get it! Do you?"* I thought as I sipped some wine from the glass in my hand.

Now, as I am feeling almost unwound, let me tell just one more.

This last summer, my spouse and I were unloading the groceries from the trunk of our car, which was parked on the driveway in front of the house. A neighbor who lives a couple of houses up the street happened to be passing along the sidewalk. He is a lonely, old man who was born and raised in this neighborhood—a distinction, indeed, if you consider the population mix around here along with the fact that this part of the town used to be, at the time of his birth, mostly empty fields.

We were kind of busy removing bags of food and household necessities, enough to fill an empty fridge and restock our depleted supplies—we had been absent for more than three months—so when we noticed Mr. Murphy standing in the middle of the driveway, obviously trying to draw our attention to himself, we became a bit annoyed.

"Hello," he said. "I haven't seen you for a while."

We tried to ignore him; however, he stubbornly continued.

"Where did you spend the summer?" he asked. "Back home?"

Wow, that was too much!

"No," I snapped. "Our home is right here. We spent time in Europe."

I was heading into the path at the end of the driveway that leads to the front door of our house, my arms full with bags, when, out of the corner of my eye, I caught a glimpse of Mr. Murphy. He was still standing, rooted to the same spot I last saw him a while ago, with a stunned expression on his face.

*"You don't get it! Do you?"* I thought as I entered the house and proceeded to the kitchen.

◆      ◆      ◆

Well, I think I will stop writing any further. I feel much better now that I have unloaded all that off my chest. The doctors are right; but, after all, they are *supposed* to be right, considering the big bucks they are getting.

So I am going to turn off the computer and stretch my aching body after spending five hours in this ergonomically wrong computer and chair set-up. You might be thinking, "Did it take you five hours to write a couple of pages of basically the same crap?" No, it did not. As a matter of fact, I had taken a break to go online and also spent some time participating in a few chat rooms and forums discussions on the Internet, arguing with people all over the world—or rather, ones who pretend to be all over the world. They all sound to me like they come from the same place as far as their warped thinking reflects the views of the same conditioned minds.

Now I am going to get ready and go to meet a friend of mine for a chat in a Yorkville café. But wait a minute. There is news over the radio about a traffic jam along University Avenue. Let me take a look at the television set.

Here they are . . . a bunch of people carrying placards and chanting slogans. Wait a minute! Where did they come from? They do not look like Canadians at all! Look at their clothes, their faces. Listen to their loud yelling. And look, there is even a spelling mistake on one of their signs! They are protesting somebody's mistreatment and insist on their human rights! My goodness, who *are* these people? Where are they from, and what do they expect? If they don't like the way they are treated here, if they are not satisfied with their lives here, they are free to go back where they came from!

I think I am beginning to feel bad anew; I am beginning to get angry all over again.

I shall have to shut off the radio, the television, *and* the computer. And as far as Yorkville is concerned, it is full of "refugees" anyway. Even my friend (or so-called friend) is not exactly a real Canadian.

I had better lie down. But before I stretch myself on the sofa, I'll go and fetch the fluffy blanket I got as a Christmas present from my so-called friend so I can cover myself from top to bottom, including my aching head. So I can hide from it all. Phew . . .

# PART TWO

PART TWO

# Report from Tel Aviv

It was a gray early afternoon in the fall of 1943.

In the center of the capital of a small Eastern European country, two men of approximately the same age walked through the wide-open doors of a church covered with light gray stones. Quickly they were swallowed by its dusky interior illuminated only by the flickering lights of candles dripping wax over brass candleholders and the golden glow of icons. The exotic smell of incense and the silence—occasionally disturbed by the muffled sound of footsteps—emitted the profound sense of serenity of a place of safety, where people could enter and find a brief reprieve from life in a world torn by hatred and destruction.

Less than an hour later, the two men were back on the street.

There was very little that distinguished one man from the other. Both were of average height, both were in their late thirties, and both wore the same conservative garb favored by professionals at that time. The only difference discernible at a glance was in their hair: the thick, curly black of one contrasted with the sparse, brown wisps of the other.

Both men seemed to be in a ponderous mood, walking rather stiffly, with thoughtful countenances on their faces. A short distance from the church, at the junction between one wide and one narrow street, they stopped.

"Thank you, Mr. Alexandrov," the one with the receding hairline said while shaking the hand of his companion.

"Don't mention it. All the best," the man with the thick, curly hair retorted. He turned into the wider street heading to a large building with stairs running along its façade ending high above the ground at a platform that lead to the massive front doors of the Palace of Justice.

The other man continued on his way, entering a labyrinth of narrow streets that cut through office buildings and apartments that rose over a variety of smaller shops and taverns on the ground floor. Piles of rubble, blown out windows, and damaged roofs blemished the view—a constant reminder of the destruction that had been inflicted on the city by recent air raids.

None of the people walking through the empty streets of this bleak city on this gray, late afternoon could imagine the future waiting for them. For now, they were concerned about nothing more than surviving: navigating through the immediate dangers lurking from the darkness of war.

◆          ◆          ◆

Ten years later, Kiril Alexandrov was walking across the square behind the church covered in light gray stones. The cluster of office buildings and apartments along the meandering narrow streets was gone, obliterated by bombs not long before the end of the war. In their place was a brand new complex of imposing, recently completed buildings, which partially filled the huge open space left by the destruction. The drastically different architecture, with its penchant for grandiose structures and huge concrete-covered open plazas, characterized the new times, and was nowhere more apparent than in this area of the city. At least for now. Dwarfed by the impregnable white stone walls that surrounded them, throngs of people with somber faces and variety of shopping bags in their hands scurried through the square.

There was determination in Mr. Alexandrov's brisk walk and in his face, which was frozen into a stoical mask. Not long before, he had suffered an irreparable blow: the end of an over twenty-five-year career and the beginning of a lifetime as a branded person in a society obsessed with distrust. Mr. Alexandrov was quick to realize that his future was a very bleak one indeed.

And then he had remembered Simeon Leviev, a former client of his, who had risen to a position of importance as a Secretary of the Party in the Ministry of Heavy Industry. It endowed him with the only power that mattered now: influence. A reference by such a man on Mr. Alexandrov's behalf could be all that was needed to grant a reversal of the decision of the authorities. Mr. Alexandrov needed help, and he was sure he would get it.

Kiril Alexandrov quickly walked to the north side of the square until he reached one of the new buildings. He stopped at its main entrance and, after a moment of hesitation, firmly pressed the palm of his right hand over the handle of the heavy door in front of him and pushed it down swiftly. Inside the marble foyer, he was confronted by a security officer staring at him with frosty eyes.

"My name is Kiril Alexandrov," he told the guard. "I have an appointment with Comrade Simeon Leviev."

After a short phone call, the officer pointed the way to Comrade Leviev's office, and followed the visitor with fixed gaze until he disappeared behind the curve that led to the stairway.

At a far end of a long room, away from the door and behind a massive desk, Comrade Leviev was seated. Hanging on the wall above him was a portrait of Josef Stalin. After a handshake and a brief exchange of pleasantries, Mr. Alexandrov came to the point, explaining his predicament and reason for calling on him.

The meeting between the two men was a cordial one. Comrade Leviev gave his consent to be mentioned in Comrade Alexandrov's appeal as a character witness. On his way out, Kiril Alexandrov's walk appeared to have acquired a good measure of lightness, and his facial expression had softened.

By contrast, as soon as the door closed behind the visitor's back, Comrade Leviev's face darkened as he plopped back into his chair with a sigh.

Those were difficult times not only for Mr. Kiril Alexandrov—who, by the way, could never get used to the new appellation of Comrade—but also for Comrade Simeon Leviev, who felt quite comfortable with this new egalitarian appendage to everybody's name, which, in spite of its ring of classless identification, had nothing to do with equality and impartiality in the distribution of power.

And it was power that was on Comrade Leviev's mind. More specifically, the fear of losing it.

Stalin's portrait was still on the wall above his head, except that after the demise of the "great leader" a few months earlier, it had become an image of a dead idol. And any reasonable man knew that living in the service and under the protection of a very powerful entity was a dangerous thing, especially when that entity ceased to exist.

Even though to most people life looked just the same now as a few months before, news was beginning to leak about startling developments far to the north, behind the Kremlin's walls. The Party members in this country were the first to know. Never feeling completely secure, Simeon Leviev felt alarmed. Especially now. His heart felt heavy with misgiving; he felt sure that he had misled Kiril Alexandrov in giving him hope by promising something he probably would not be able to deliver.

He felt sorry for Mr. Alexandrov as well as for himself.

Only a couple of weeks later, Comrade Simeon Leviev had become a casualty of the shake up in the Party. Maybe he failed to take down Stalin's portrait quickly enough, or maybe he was just losing his faith in an idea that had so inspired him as a young student, thus weakening his focus and rendering him sloppy in letting his guard down at a moment when the Party was taking a turn—a time requiring utmost vigilance.

Meanwhile, Mr. Alexandrov had lost his resolve for filing the appeal and had faced reality. Not a single petition had resulted in reversal of the initial decision. His walk had lost its short-lived suppleness, and the stoical expression had returned to his face, now hardened even further.

The two men did not see each other anymore. That is to say that many years would have to go by till they would meet again.

Meanwhile, they both moved on, each enduring and surviving, enclosed in world of his own. And each step along the way, each time faith presented them with a situation that required making the slightest choice, it was hard—sometimes excruciatingly painful. For everyone's life was hanging on a string, and all of those strings were attached to the hands of a very few people whose own lives were on even shorter strings, attached at the top to the fingers of a single pair of hands—one very powerful pair of hands.

But neither man ever lost hope, for this is human nature—at least up to a point.

Quite independent of one another, these two men happened to have very similar families. Mr. Alexandrov had a son and so did Mr. Leviev (by now he did not feel comfortable being called Comrade).

Life for Bojidar Alexandrov, Mr. Alexandrov's son, was not easy. There was always a price to be paid by the children for the transgressions—real or imaginary— of their parents and grandparents. That's just the way it was.

However, Bojidar eventually succeeded at getting into the university and graduated with a degree in civil engineering. At the end of his studies, though, he found himself facing a bleak future. The diploma in his pocket was not enough to open the tightly shut doors to opportunities for his kind. So, eventually, he came to the conclusion that his only option, although a risky one, was to get away from this place. To the chagrin of his parents, nonetheless with their blessing, he fled to the West in search of a new, better life.

On the other hand, Simeon Leviev's son, Emil, had shown a talent in linguistics by mastering several languages—a skill that blended well with his aptitude for writing. However, he could never manage to get far as a writer, never been able to find the right formula for creating an acceptable piece of work. All he wrote was deemed too personal, reeking of decadence and bordering on dangerous. Emil had finally found a job as the editor of a magazine that focused on women's issues, the emphasis being on cooking recipes and knitting patterns. It was a good position for many, but less-than-satisfactory for a young man endowed with Emil's creative and ambitious spirit.

His parents helplessly watched their son languish unfulfilled and miserable, often commiserating with him, all the while torn apart inside by the conviction that they had somehow failed him.

Alexandrov and Leviev were growing old, and were beginning to take stock of their lives. They remembered the world through weary eyes and ponderings. But is this what all older people do, or merely the tired ones?

Almost thirty-five years had elapsed since the two men had seen each other when they met again. And it was for the last time, indeed. They still looked very similar—except for their hair, of course.

Mr. Alexandrov had been brought back home after a short stay in a hospital for treatment of a serious illness. He had lost his wife a couple of years earlier and had been living alone until he had fallen ill. Now he was taken care of by a sister many years his junior.

He was released from the hospital not because he was doing well and was recuperating, but because the doctors had come to the contrary conclusion that there was no hope for Mr. Alexandrov ever to recover. So, in accordance with practice regarding old people and hopeless cases, he was sent home. Letting people expire in hospitals was a bad policy, for there were plans to be fulfilled, achievements to be reported and boasted about, and statistics to be compared. Friendships, devotion, loyalties, even lives, were all supposed to last forever. But who would be proud of the natural death of an ordinary person?

So Mr. Alexandrov had been sent home to wait out the end of his life, bedridden in the corner of a small room cluttered with old furniture: chairs, a rickety table, and a wobbly bookcase filled with old books with covers soiled by the polluted air drifting through the open window. Wooden boxes attached to the windowsills hung precariously over the sidewalk six stories below. Clumps of drooping petunias broke the monotony of the outside view, which was obscured by the gray stone facade of a building across the street.

Kiril Alexandrov was alone in the room, oblivious of the intermittent sound of water dripping from a tap into a chipped cast-iron sink that stood in the opposite corner of the room. A sharp doorbell ring reverberated through the small apartment and summoned Mr. Alexandrov's sister from the adjacent room to the entrance hall. Energetically, she flung the door open. A short, shabby man dressed in worn-out pants and an open-neck, short-sleeved shirt was standing in front of the doorway. He was holding a cloth shopping bag in his right hand. There was something touching about his demeanor.

"Would you allow me to see Mr. Alexandrov?" the man asked.

He spoke in a soft voice. His manner was hesitant, yet very polite and so tentative, Mr. Alexandrov's sister thought. Being a bit hard of hearing, she had to strain her ears to catch his words. She understood that the man was, rather had been once upon a time, her brother's client. However, he had not been in touch with Mr. Alexandrov for a very, very long time.

He explained that through a mutual acquaintance, he had learned about the former lawyer's very serious illness and wanted to see him before it was too late— the last sentiment, of course, was merely implied. Also, he had a compelling reason to talk to Mr. Alexandrov, and the pleading look in his eyes made that point quite obvious. For Mr. Alexandrov's sister, who considered herself a good judge of character and felt sure that the man was sincere, there was no cause to mistrust him.

"Well, come in," she said, pushing the door out as far as it would go while stepping aside, letting the man squeeze by.

Inside the small entrance foyer, she pointed to the room straight ahead and led him to the bed where Mr. Alexandrov was lying under a light blanket.

"Kiril, here is a client of yours," she said. "He came to pay you a visit."

The sick man did not show any signs of recognition after glancing at the figure standing next to his bed. Still, it was indifference rather than the absence of mind that his eyes conveyed.

Mr. Alexandrov's sister pulled a chair next to the bed, took the cloth shopping bag from the old man, and placed it on the table close by. Then she turned around and headed for the door, stopping for a moment on her way out to tighten the loose tap in a fruitless effort to stop the dripping water. As she left the small room, she pulled the door closed behind her, leaving the two men alone.

Half an hour later, she heard the muffled noise of measured steps coming from the entrance hall and rushed to send off the guest, who was already waiting by the apartment's front door.

"Thank you, Madam" the old man muttered as he passed through the doorway, the cloth shopping bag in his hand.

"Good-bye, sir," Mr. Alexandrov's sister called out from behind the stooped back of the slow moving man at the top of the descending stairs.

Back inside, filled with curiosity, she went to check on her brother. She found him in the same position in which she had left him earlier: his arms pulled over the blanket resting on his chest, his eyes shut and lips tight. Carefully, she walked out the room, pulled the door closed and moved as quietly as she could to the adjacent room.

A few hours later, Mr. Alexandrov looked much livelier, refreshed and talkative. His sister brought up the topic of the visitor.

"Kiril, who was your afternoon visitor?" she asked. "Have never seen him before."

"No wonder," he replied. "I haven't seen him for a long time either."

Mr. Alexandrov loved his sister; he did not mean to snap at her.

"He was an old client," he said, then paused. "Actually, more of a friend. But from a very long time ago."

"Simeon something?" his sister asked.

"Simeon Leviev," Mr. Alexandrov clarified.

"What did you talk about?" blurted his sister.

"What indeed," he said. "First, he thanked me, and then he said he was not sure if it was the right thing he did."

Mr. Alexandrov's sister seemed greatly puzzled.

"What are you talking about, Kiril?" she asked.

Mr. Alexandrov had closed his eyes, overcome by fatigue.

"I became his godfather in 1943."

With a worried look in her eyes, his sister stared at her brother in silence.

"His name was Solomon Levy. His family had heard the rumors. He came to the office; we talked. He asked for advice."

A glimpse of a smirk crossed Mr. Alexandrov's face.

"I was a lawyer," he added. "Someone to be trusted . . ."

His sister's reaction was swift.

"Did he upset you? Did he blame you? It was his choice, wasn't it? You were only trying to help, weren't you?"

Noticing her brother's grimace, she continued apologetically.

"He looks so nice and meek," she said. "If I had known he would upset you, I wouldn't have invited him in."

Her brother listened without interrupting her outburst, with the same feeling of satisfaction he felt every time he felt reassured of her love and devotion. Finally, he closed his eyes again,

"Sis, do not fret," he said. "He did not upset me at all."

As she left the room, Mr. Alexandrov's sister thought she heard him muttering, "He must be getting tired."

She hesitated for an instant, wondering if she should turn around and ask what he meant. Then she reconsidered; hard of hearing as she was, she was not sure whether she had actually heard anything at all. Anyway, there was no point in carrying the conversation any further. Kiril had had enough excitement for one day.

◆          ◆          ◆

In the late summer of 2001, the attention of the few thousand viewers of *The Morning Show* of the ever popular All News Television Network was suddenly drawn to a high level of anticipation by large, bold notice appearing on the bottom of the television screens. It read BREAKING NEWS.

The ongoing program at the moment was an interview with a well-respected scholar from a reputable university with impressive credentials and profound knowledge on the Middle East. He was expounding on his views of the prospects for peace in the troubled region. The anchorperson had to abruptly cut the conversation short to announce that the network was switching from the studio schedule to a live report from the location of the dramatic events developing at this very moment.

The image on the screen changed to an outdoor shot of a reporter holding a microphone in front of her face. She was standing in the middle of a chaotic, gruesome scene on a street in Tel Aviv, just minutes after an explosion had been heard: the latest suicide bombing.

The powerful blast had ripped a bus shelter to smithereens. A few times, the camera moved away from the reporter to show a glimpse of a destroyed car, dazed people limping with bloodstained clothes, wandering around until intercepted by the efficient, fast-moving paramedics on the scene. Quick rotation of the camera and the lens focused briefly on a victim being taken away on a stretcher by four running men. With a small downward tilt of the camera, one could see red spots on the pavement and a heap covered with blue plastic with a shoe sticking out of it. It was presumably the body of the suicide bomber—or what was left of it.

The reports were still preliminary. It was obvious from the pictures that there were many casualties. There were no confirmations pertaining to the exact number of dead, which stood at least at half a dozen. For the moment.

Later that same day, the first item on the late-night newscast on a local television station in a large Canadian city was a report on the sudden death of a respectable businessman, Mr. Bojidar Alexandrov, who had been on a business trip to Tel Aviv. He was known in the community as an associate in a construction company with headquarters in the city. Mr. Alexandrov had become a victim of the earlier-reported suicide bombing. An innocent victim like the rest, the tragedy became even more poignant considering the fact that he was a foreigner from far-away place, who was in no way connected to the history of the grievances of the inhabitants of this contested land—clearly a case of the wrong man in the wrong place in the wrong time.

Included in the news segment was a small detail of the story revealed by the son of Bojidar Alexandrov: the businessman was killed on his way to a meeting with an old classmate from the country of his birth who now lived in Israel. In the eyes of the anchorman, this circumstance seemed to have added to the absurdity of this tragedy.

In conclusion, the anchorman said that Mr. Bojidar Alexandrov, who had left behind a wife, Cindy, a son, Cyril, and daughter, Jennifer, would be sadly missed by the whole community. According to the testament of a neighbor of the family, interviewed earlier, that was indeed the case.

Meanwhile, back in Tel Aviv, in a café not far from the site of the bombing that had taken place the previous day, an elderly man sat at a table reading a newspaper. The thin edition, only a couple of pages long, was trembling in the grip of his knobby hands. The man's attention was drawn to a family picture of a couple of teenagers with their parents standing behind them; their hands placed on their children's shoulders. Below the photo ran an article about the story of one of the victims of the suicide bombing.

Emil Levy, along with his wife Mya and their children, Solomon and Sara, had immigrated to Israel less than a year earlier. The elderly man empathized with the family of Emil, who had been born and raised in the same small, mountainous country by the Black Sea from which he himself had come. It had been more than forty years since the elderly man had made the same journey, but he still remembered it fondly. As a matter of fact, so did the many Jewish immigrants from this same country, many of who had settled in Tel Aviv. Throughout the years they had kept their native language, prepared their grandmothers' dishes, fretted over the unavailability of garlic, played soccer, acquired a reputation for leaning to the left in their political views, and kept in touch by sending packages of food or clothes to people they hardly knew anymore.

The article about the Levy family was one of several, none of which were particularly long and thorough as far as details went about each family's background. Just an ordinary story about ordinary immigrants, with one difference—they had just lost the provider, the father of two teenagers.

The old man's thoughts drifted. Perhaps, he thought, this man was the son of somebody he knew, of a childhood friend. And the way it had happened seemed to strike a soft spot in the elderly man's heart; Emil Levy was on the way to meet an old classmate on a business trip from a far-away country when the shrapnel from the exploding bomb had entered his body and pierced his heart, killing him instantly.

The tremor of the elderly man's hands had turned into an uncontrollable shake. Hastily, he put down the newspaper and leaned heavily against the back of his chair. His whole body was overcome by a sudden fatigue while his mind wondered,

*"What is wrong with the world? When is all this going to end?"*

This certainly was not the first sad story the old man had read. He had seen much and he had experienced plenty during his long life.

Yet, there were things he still could not get used to.

# Memories in Stone

On a bench constructed from heavy wooden planks supported by concrete pillars, a slender old man rested. His leathery, sunburned face was furrowed with deep wrinkles. The transparent, milky film covering his gray eyes softened their once piercing look. Presently, they were fixed on a boy swirling around on a skateboard over a concrete-covered square. The youngster was his great-grandson.

A huge monument standing at the far end of a commemorative complex towered above the landscape, throwing its protective shadow over the bench and the old man. The foreground of the eighty-foot-long mall was flanked by massive stone-covered platforms, each a couple of meters tall. On top of each one was a display of larger-than-life groups of figures of robust peasants and workers handing fruits and flowers to smiling soldiers. The figures on top of the obelisk—more than ten meters tall, and the focal point of the complex—depicted a soldier, a peasant-woman, and a worker standing by. Their gaze, high above ground, was directed toward the future: a reassuring message, in the spirit of the time during which the memorial was built.

The pinnacle of the monolithic structure was poignantly outlined by the very tip of a submachine gun sticking out of the warrior's arm raised in triumph. A number of steps running across the entire width of the square broke the monotony of the flat concrete surface, while adding to the oppressive grandeur of all that stone.

Quite appropriately, for this was the monument to the Red Army—built to commemorate the glory of a foreign army by a grateful regime that was brought in and protected by its might for forty-five years. The regime was gone, but the symbol remained.

For the old man, this was a place where he could escape from the present and remember. Once, he had power; he had been a "somebody." He had a wife and two boys. The wife had died, and his boys had grown up into men with wives, with children of their own. The young lad he had brought to this place today was generations removed from him, but blood is thicker than water, as the saying goes.

It had transformed the once-fierce colonel into a benevolent great-grandfather who found solace only in his memories and in this boy.

Here, in the shadow of the monument, his memories were good.

A benign smile crossed his face.

"Bravo Mitko!" he called out. "You are amazing!"

He tempered his encouragement with caution:

"Watch out! Don't do that!"

Mitko was racing across the square, heading straight toward the stairs, following other kids who were showing off their skills by doing flips and going up and down the steps.

"Ah, the boy has courage!" thought the old soldier, as he observed his great-grandson zoom over the concrete steps, the sculptured heroic figures looming high above him in the background.

Over the noise of children's shrieks and the rumble of roller skates and skateboards, the sound of an accordion was audible. Another not-so-old man, sitting on a stool just below the stairs, was playing a string of old melodies reminiscent of the war fought by the soldiers immortalized in stone.

"Ah, the memories . . . the fights we fought! The battles we won against the enemies! And they were numerous and everywhere!"

The old man's chest swelled with emotion and moisture crept into his eyes. The heat was getting to him, or so he thought.

Suddenly, he felt tired. It was late afternoon and they had to get going. Mitko's parents would be back from work and would expect to find them at home.

"Grandpa, will we come back tomorrow?" the boy said, with a hint of pleading in his voice.

"Yes, my son. But first, let us see what your parents have to say about that."

Actually, the old man was eager to leave the city and return to his native village where he had gradually reestablished himself after his wife's death a few years earlier. He had done well during his career. He had led a good life and had secured the future of his children and even grandchildren. At least this is what he had in mind when he acquired not one or two, but three apartments, all located in close proximity to each other. For a while, as a widower, he tried to live by himself. However, he finally realized that this new lifestyle did not suit him—a conclusion shaped to a degree by the pressure exerted on him by one of his sons.

It had to do with living accommodations. His older son and daughter-in-law shared their two-bedroom apartment with their married son's family, while the old man lived all by himself—a luxury, from most people's point of view. The old man relented and ended up spending most of the year in his ancestral home in a village about sixty kilometers from the city; although, he kept moving back to weather the cold winter months in more comfortable conditions. Fortunately, he was in remarkably good health for his eighty-five years.

During summertime, his trips to the city were short, few, and far-between; just long enough to collect his pension, buy some medicine, and see his favorite great-grandchild. When in the city, he always came to the memorial to spend a few hours reflecting and recharging his spirit.

At the end of that particular afternoon, as enjoyable as it was, the old man was beginning to feel the urge to return to his village, to his life of independence, self-reliance, and the serenity of nature.

"We shall see, my son," he said. "Wait till tomorrow." He reiterated his previous statement in less convincing terms, reducing it from nearly a promise to more of a possibility.

Hand-in-hand, the old man and the boy—clutching his skate-board under his other arm—headed toward the bus stop to catch a ride home.

As their bus receded in the distance, a taxi traveling in the opposite direction came to a stop close to the bus shelter. A sprightly couple got off.

Elena and Peter had come back for a visit to their native country after thirty-five years of absence. Now in their early sixties, they were filled with excitement and anticipation, muted only by an attempt to put things into perspective.

*Certainly, things would have changed; a long time has passed. But, after all, once this was home, and in a way, it always was!*

They had arrived only the day before. It had been a long journey, thousands of miles over the ocean, mountains, and valleys—quilts of neat patches of land in different shades of green, brown and yellow—seen through the breaks in the whirling clouds surrounding the plane high in the sky.

Today was the first day of their visit to the city, and they had decided to spend it strolling along one of their favorite places: a boulevard paved with yellow bricks, with a pedestrian strip in the middle and lined with chestnut trees. The entire area comprised of unique buildings which housed the most important governmental and educational institutions, churches, and memorials—testimonials to the past and symbols of the most cherished values of the nation, erected in gardens and squares. It provided the post card view of the capital. For anybody searching, wandering, or torn between two worlds, this was the place to find some answers—especially on a sunny day, drenched in languid southern warmth, when it was easy to foster optimism and sustain excitement.

As it happened, today was one of those days. What a good idea it was, to take this walk right now, Elena and Peter thought. They would call upon distant cousins and old friends later.

So they hired a taxi to the Eagle's Bridge, got out at the intersection between the boulevard by the river and the boulevard paved with yellow bricks, and started walking. Hardly a hundred feet down the road, they came upon the site of the commemorative complex. They stopped.

"What is that?" Elena asked. "There used to be a garden there surrounded by a wrought-iron fence."

"The zoo was behind it," Peter added. "It isn't there anymore, is it?"

Both retreated to the corner to get a clearer view from the other side of the complex, to see if there were some remnants of what they had remembered. There was nothing but open space and dirt, covered by poorly maintained greenery.

"Remember, there was a wall running along this stretch of the street?" Elena said, pointing out into the distance. "And right there were the cages for the wolves and the hyenas."

Now she was pointing to the edge of the square, grimacing.

"I remember the stench," she said. After a pause, she wondered aloud, "Where did the animals go?"

"To a different location, to a new zoo, I suppose," remarked Peter.

Back in front of the monument, Elena grew even more astonished.

"Monument to the Red Army!" she blurted. "One wouldn't expect to see such a monstrosity now."

"It is not as though somebody really cares for it," Peter added, pointing to the colorful graffiti that defaced the sides of the pedestals as well as the base of the main monument: slogans, acronyms for a variety of political parties, sports clubs, even profanities in a foreign language expressing enthusiastic support for, or vehement opposition to, all of these entities.

Vandalism, or a forum for free expression of opinion? Disturbed, Elena and Peter turned away from the sight and continued their walk along the boulevard. That proved to be a considerable challenge.

The sidewalks, as well as the pedestrian island, were impassible, jammed by tightly parked cars that were wedged into each other so closely that it made one wonder how the drivers would ever be able to extricate their vehicles. Pedestrians navigated through the maze, mindful of the speeding, chaotic traffic on the street, perpetually watching the flow of vehicles with obvious apprehension every time they had to step down from the sidewalk in order to bypass a parked car. Merely advancing along was a tedious and slow task; sightseeing was a dangerous distraction.

Finally able to squeeze through this stretch of the boulevard, and greatly relieved, Elena and Peter found themselves in the clearing around the monument of Alexander the Second of Russia. An old, familiar site, once a favorite hangout for teenagers, referred to as the place "behind the horse's tail." The mere thought of all those idle hours spent there, puffing on cigarettes and contemplating the great mysteries of life—a euphemism for sex and juicy gossip—brought smiles to their faces. Those were good memories!

The flowers and green shrubbery that surrounded the handsomely proportionate monument of the Tsar Liberator evoked feeling of coziness felt long ago . . . And there was the splendid sculpture. His posture straight and dignified, his horse's legs planted firmly on the pedestal in a moment of complete repose, the Tsar Liberator's gaze appeared to be fixed on the golden domes of the Alexander Nevsky Cathedral sparkling in the brilliant light of the afternoon sun: another memorial built by a grateful nation to the glory of liberation.

Alas, the pleasant thoughts and warm feelings were not to last. Just a little farther down, on the opposite side of the road, more unfamiliar sights brought uneasiness and wonderment. A startling statue of a tall, gaunt man wearing long, loose garb, his arms outstretched and his face uplifted, its chiseled features bearing resemblance to no one and to all, begged questions: Martyr, hero, or saint? Most probably, all of the above. Defiant or tragic? Most probably, both. Meant to inspire, or a sad cry of lamentation evoking pity? It was hard to tell. The statue had been erected in a small park. More similar sculptures were scattered among patches of flaming-red rose bushes.

So many monuments, so many victims, so many bad memories . . .

Elena and Peter were getting tired. In search of a place to rest, they kept walking until they came across the Military Garden opposite the Military Club—a humble hallmark of forgotten glory. Weather-beaten wooden benches lined the paved path running diagonally across the green. The asphalt was blotched by cracks and potholes—another old, familiar sight. The small park was located at the junction of the boulevard and a wide street once known as the drag by the young people of generations past. Now it seemed deserted.

Inside the garden, on a spot surrounded by freshly disturbed soil, a new, still-shiny sculpture demanded attention. With interest, Elena and Peter approached a massive bust set on a low platform. A huge crack cut deep into the skull. A plaque displayed near the monument stated that this was a memorial dedicated to Stambolov, assassinated more than one hundred years earlier. He had been a head of state—a most skillful and able politician; once famous for his foresight and dedication, later rejected and obliterated from the pages of history. Now, in search of untarnished heroes, he had been dug out from the past and remembered. Not as a statesman and leader, but just as another victim. There it was: one more sad sob, one more bitter tear.

As Elena and Peter stood nearby contemplating, a much younger man, in his early forties, shabbily dressed and wearing a dour expression on his face, stopped and stared at the statue.

Without hesitation, and with much bitterness, he remarked, "Bastards! Hacked him to death. The fascists!"

Puzzled by the last reference indicating a more recent past, Peter turned to the man.

"You are talking about Stamboliisky, aren't you? This is not Stamboliisky," he said. "This is Stambolov."

His face expressing incredulity mixed with confusion, the man snapped, "Who?"

Without inquiring further, waving his hand in a dismissive gesture, the man turned around and went on his way. It was not clear to whom his disdain was directed—against this new hero or against this calm, formal-looking couple who awoke in him the suspicion and resentment he felt toward strangers. And there was no doubt in his mind that those two were outsiders; he could almost smell their foreignness. Never mind what language they spoke.

By now, Peter and Elena were exhausted. The two dropped onto the nearest empty bench. To their right, the old Military Club looked reassuringly unchanged.

"Mother used to tell me about the balls she attended there," Elena recalled sadly while looking with affection at the freshly repainted façade of the comely building.

Following her gaze, Peter remarked, "The army paraded in front of it on the feast of Saint George. Father told me a story . . ."

He went on telling the old story in a voice reverberating with the same pride with which his father had related it to him as a young child. During a parade, turning his head to face the Tsar and the dignitary reviewing the troops, a soldier impaled himself on the tip of the bayonet resting against his shoulder. He did not flinch. He raised his hand in a salute and, without missing a beat, kept on marching. It was only when somebody noticed the blood streaming down his face did people realized he had been injured.

There was no end to the story—one had to assume that the brave soldier had not been left to bleed to death. But this was a story with a message: "Once, we were a disciplined, tough, and proud people, who indulged in colorful pomp and pageantry like any Western civilized nation. Accordingly, we shared the same values."

Meanwhile, Elena's eyes had moved to the left and remained fixed on an old tree, its branches, thick and numerous, spread over a wide area. As soon as Peter finished his narrative, Elena turned back to him.

"Do you remember this tree?" she asked.

Nonplussed, Peter did not answer.

"Its branches used to be covered with sparrows. Thousands of them! It was kind of phenomenon. The newspapers wrote about it." After a pause, she smiled. "A risky business, passing under the tree, it was."

Growing agitated, Elena started looking around. On a bench next to them, there was a woman seating all by herself. Elena leaned toward her and asked politely, pointing out to the old tree, "Excuse me, madam. Can you tell me what happened to the sparrows? The ones that used to live on that tree, over there."

"What sparrows?" the woman inquired. The expression on her face clearly indicated apprehension.

"There were so many, covering all the branches so densely that the tree would turn brown," Elena said. "They made lots of noise also, chirping all day long. I remember them very well!"

"I have been living here for twenty years and I have never seen any sparrows on that tree," the woman said. After this obvious exaggeration, she added, "Except for all those dirty pigeons. They are everywhere, messing up everything."

Reconsidering something, the woman shifted to a friendlier tone.

"When was that?" she asked Elena.

Elena pulled herself away.

"Oh, it was long, very long ago."

Like most couples who had spent most of their lives together, Elena and Peter had acquired the uncanny faculty to share the same thoughts without communicating them in words. Now, both fell into a melancholy silence.

*"This walk was not a good idea,"* Peter thought.

*"Where did the sparrows go?"* Elena wondered.

Incessantly searching for food—pecking at the gravel, the grass, and every bit of garbage strewn about—the droves of slightly pompous pigeons kept stalking closer and closer to Elena and Peter's feet. Both, though, seemed completely unaware of their presence, but for one. A particularly large specimen of the pesky birds stood still, perched on top of Stambolov's head, right on the edge of the crack that split his skull. Seemingly mesmerized by the sluggishly moving whitish blob creeping down the temple of the face, Elena and Peter murmured in unison.

"Dirty scavengers! Messing up everything!"

# The Transformation of the Village of Kriva Gusha

Nobody knows when the village of Kriva Gusha* came into existence, where its settlers drifted from, or what prompted them to give it such a strange name. This is a moot point, though, as there are quite a few villages in the area bearing names just as weird as this one; names that read like the index of an anatomy textbook: Rebro**, Garlo***, Krivonoss****.

However, there is one thing that everybody knows for sure: for centuries this entire region had been trampled by hordes of people moving from east to west and back.

The testaments of the area's history are sparse: a few Roman roads and knolls scattered over the fields sometimes referred to by the natives as "The Jerusalem Cemeteries." But the lack of material vestiges from centuries of forgotten, or rather neglected bygones does not mean that there are no other intangible traces of them. The mystic past lurks everywhere—from the obvious to the subtle—from the physical appearance of the locals to their deep-rooted beliefs.

Throughout the years, the village of Kriva Gusha underwent a few changes, although they had never amounted to a profound metamorphosis. So for better or worse, it never really caught up with the modern world.

And if anything, this brought some charm to the place.

At dawn, on the day of the feast of the Holy Spirit, Ivanka woke up covered in perspiration with her heart wildly racing in her chest. She had been startled from a nightmare: walking along a road that had suddenly turned into a quagmire of slippery, sticky mud that had swallowed her feet quickly. Then, horrified, she had

---

\*      *Crooked Neck*
\*\*     *Rib*
\*\*\*    *Throat*
\*\*\*\*  *Crooked Nose*

seen the shining headlights of a large truck heading straight at her. Frantically, she had struggled to extricate herself from the gooey mire until, at last, she had succeeded escaping a terrible fate by rolling away from the path of the monster's unrelenting march.

Now wide-awake, she found herself seated in bed, leaning on the sweaty palms of her hands, her eyes wandering in confusion until she fixed them on the open window and caught a glimpse of the pale blue sky. She felt the fresh air that pushed through the sheer curtains caressing her face. She heard the rumble of the nearby brook and the songs of the nightingales, and she realized that it all was just a bad dream. Swiftly she pulled herself up, threw her legs over the side of the bed, and reaching the floor with her bare feet, shoved them into the knitted slippers neatly left there the night before. By the time she got dressed, she was in complete control of her faculties.

Long before, Ivanka had made up her mind to go to the annual fair in the town of Dubovo. The day finally had come—the feast of the Holy Spirit—so she got busy. She had a score of chores in and around the house that needed to be taken care of in time to catch the bus heading to Dubovo. All the while she was shuttling between the barn, the cowshed, and the chicken coop, she felt an uneasiness growing deep inside her, a foreboding feeling creeping out from the dark images lodged in her sub-consciousness. What was the meaning of the dream? She was not sure, but she was certain of one thing: it was a bad omen.

Dubovo was surrounded by rolling hills outlined against a chain of mountain peaks that spread out in the faraway distance. The town was the administrative center for a cluster of small villages, often hidden from view, just off the main highway. It was a cozy little town whose ambiance, at late, had been improved considerably by a string of outside cafés that had sprung up along the shady sidewalks of its curved main thoroughfare and its spacious square. People went there to enjoy their first espresso and to read the daily news in the fresh coolness of the early morning hours. Later, mothers pushing baby carriages went there to share their second espresso with friends. And everybody went there in the evening to have a last cup of coffee or a shot of brandy with family and friends. In the early afternoon hours, however, all cafés were empty, save for occasional travelers taking a break. For a couple of hours, the whole town appeared deserted. It was no wonder life in Dubovo was flowing at a slow pace. Nobody was in a hurry there. And all day long, its citizens meandered through the streets of their town in quite a leisurely manner, ignoring the speeding cars that whistled through the thoroughfares.

A few days before the feast of the Holy Spirit, the sleepy little town of Dubovo was teeming with activity in preparation for the upcoming celebration. Crews of Romies—a newly accepted term referring to the gypsies—armed with brooms and shovels diligently swept the streets. Trucks loaded with shiny, silvery street lamps were unloaded and expediently mounted, replacing the old rusty ones. The stone wall that surrounded the park underwent long-overdue repairs, and was fitted with brand new wooden benches in recesses specially created for that purpose. In the town's main square, workers busily installed carousels and Ferris wheels.

Dubovo was transformed into a squeaky-clean, picture-perfect small town in time for the feast. Even the potholes on the highway and the main street were filled, ensuring a smooth ride for the expected throng of visitors. And especially for one very important visitor: it was rumored that the president of the republic himself was coming—a local boy who had made it good!

The big day was pleasantly warm and cheerfully sunny. The vendors in the square were all doing brusque business. The cafés were packed.

Meanwhile, the official part of the celebration was underway. In the park, standing on a wooden podium, a tall, handsome man was delivering a speech. A small crowd of people was on hand to cheer him on. This was not the president; unfortunately, he had been prevented from attending the feast by more pressing governmental matters. In his place, an official had been sent from his office.

The platform had been erected in front of a gray stone monument that was flanked by a couple of freshly painted antique artillery guns placed there long before internationalism and worker's brotherhood were elevated to inspirational status. Now, once again, patriotism was in vogue. Away from the park, in the town square, the white-stone statue of a woman partisan stood ignored and neglected. The mighty figure, crowned with a splendid mane of hair covered with patches of green mold, blended quite well with the colorful scenery.

Standing in the midst of the crowd, Ivanka strained to hear some of the words coming in chopped fragments over the crackling microphone. Like everybody else there, she was somewhat disappointed. She had come to see the president, not somebody she had never heard of before. Though she was willing to give the man a chance.

Ivanka had been born and raised in Kriva Gusha, but she had married a man from Dubovo and had spent half of her life in the town, working and raising a family. A few years earlier, her husband had passed away and she had moved back to the village. The apartment had become too small for her and her married daughter, who by now had a couple of children of her own. Besides, life in Kriva Gusha was cheaper and less-stressful.

A slight tap on Ivanka's shoulder made her turn around.

"Sis?" The call of recognition was said in a low voice, almost a whisper.

"Dragomir?" she replied.

A stocky man in his late thirties or early forties stood right next to her. His eyes seemed fixed in a permanent stare. Under his loose T-shirt, a thick gold chain hanging around his neck shone with a yellow glow.

Ivanka felt a sudden pang in her chest and a tug at her heart.

"When did you get here?" she asked, surprised. "Are you alone?"

"I'm alone, and I need your help," he replied.

Dragomir's voice was soft, like before; nevertheless, Ivanka understood: this was a command rather than a request.

She knew her little brother, the youngest of her siblings, well. When he was born, she was into her teens—old enough to help with raising him. Through the years her devotion had developed into a great affection, almost a weakness, for the little tyke. Unfortunately, the unruly, though charming boy grew into a reckless, irresponsible man. A failed marriage, estranged children, jail time, some shady business ventures—all were part of his life story. Still, Ivanka would do anything she could for him; all he had to do was just ask.

And that he did often.

"Leave the gate open tonight," he said. "I'll be there,"

Then he disappeared into the crowd.

Ivanka's zeal for the fair had drained away. She wished she was back home. Troubled and anxious, her head was beginning to hurt from the endless questions she kept asking herself in vain. She wondered *What to do now?* Dragomir had vanished without a trace, and there was plenty of time to kill before the scheduled bus ride for her return home. Carefully, Ivanka made her way out of the crowd and, after a short hesitation, took a turn toward the outskirts of the town, leading to the green hill at the end of a short side street.

Back in Kriva Gusha later that night, the inhabitants of a neat, white cottage located at the opposite end of the village from Ivanka's home were surprised to see an unfamiliar car parked in front of their house. They had spent the evening reading and listening to the radio without paying attention to the passing time. And why should they? A retired couple, they had bought the small house on an impulse after a very pleasant drive through the area. As luck would have it, they had passed through Kriva Gusha and were taken by the natural beauty and peacefulness of its surroundings. They had inquired about the availability of an affordable place, and to their surprise, were told that there were many abandoned, empty houses. So Mr. and Mrs. Dimitrov bought one of those dirt-cheap properties—a small, slightly dilapidated cottage with a neglected, but still lovely, garden—did some renovations and became a permanent presence during the summertime.

Maria and Nicolai Dimitrovs were city folk with somewhat romantic notions about village life. And since the locals never warmed up to them—they never did to outsiders—they remained ignorant strangers who saw things differently than their native neighbors.

That night, the road in front of the Dimitrov household was pitch black. There was no light coming from the moonless, overcast sky above to dispel the darkness. Maria and Nicolai's attention was drawn to the outside only by the sudden sound of a running motor. Intrigued, they went to investigate.

The pale light cast by the outside lamp did not reach far beyond the doorway they were standing in. No matter how hard they strained their eyes, they could not distinguish more than a shadow of a man fussing about a boxy, light-colored car parked by the iron fence in front of their house.

"Looking for somebody?" Maria inquired cordially.

"Umm, just visiting friends," the man replied without facing them, still standing by the car. "Do you mind if I leave the car here? Just for a while."

"Of course not," Nicolai said, just as cordially as his wife.

"Good-night," the stocky, soft-spoken man said as he began to walk away.

"Good-night," echoed the couple while closing the door.

"Have you ever seen that guy?" Nicolai asked.

"No. Seems a nice fellow, though. Wonder who he is visiting." Maria's voice was brimming with curious excitement.

"A young widow or a divorcee, perhaps?" Nicolai said.

They never saw the man again, but did observe the same car parked on the same spot several times during the next few weeks. It usually appeared late in the evening and was always gone by daybreak. As soon as one of the Dimitrovs spotted the car, the other was informed cheerfully: "the lover-boy is here."

Somehow, that made them feel good, like coconspirators with a stake in a little romantic mischief.

To say that there had not been big changes in the village of Kriva Gusha would be misleading. More than fifty years earlier, a great calamity had befallen the villagers: the land had been taken away from the peasants. But what is a peasant without land? And what is a village without peasants?

There was land to toil in the cooperatives. As in a city factory, there was machinery, there were plans to fulfill, and there were schedules to follow. But what kind of life was that for a peasant? Like any hand for hire, nothing really tied him to the village. At any time he felt free to pick up his suitcase and leave the village and its joyless drudgery of peasant life. And it was not as though he was going to be missed. The plowing would be done, the crops would be harvested, and the herds would be taken to pasture. The land and the cattle—none were his.

Then, suddenly, the system collapsed and another big change occurred. The cooperatives were dismantled, all machinery was looted in the ensuing confusion, and finally, the land was to be given back. But to whom, and how?

The city folk in high places were in a hurry and did not, or could not, come up with anything better than a very confusing scheme. People made claims based on old deeds, then brought a couple of witnesses to verify the boundaries of the land they claimed, and voila—they were issued brand new deeds. And where, after more than forty years, would witnesses who still remembered the boundaries of every piece of land be found? Apparently in a couple of octogenarians, who for a while were the most courted and merry old people around.

So all that goes around eventually comes around. Not quite, though. The village that had once boasted more than a thousand inhabitants had been reduced to fewer than one hundred registered citizens. During the summer, the population swelled by about a hundred people, but as the new school year loomed, the tide would again subside. The children who had left years earlier did not come back to toil the repossessed land of their fathers and grandfathers, and the abandoned fields turned into meadows. It created a pretty picture for the visitors, but a bleak one for the few remaining peasants who stubbornly stuck to their way of life.

A narrow, steep road off the main highway led up to the village of Kriva Gusha. On both sides of it, behind the rows of rosehip bushes outlining it, stretched meadows as far as the eye could see. It was a pretty picture, indeed.

Sporting a wide-brimmed straw hat, floral cotton dress, and rubber boots, Ivanka strode down the road on her way to a small patch of land that she had turned into a vegetable garden. Growing and preserving vegetables had become a national obsession: an absolute necessity for many as well as a compulsion for a few. A large bag hung over her left arm for the zucchini and onions ready for the picking. In her right arm, she carried a brown ornate wooden staff, its bark covered with whimsical figures.

"One has to carry a stick always, one never knows when it might be needed," Ivanka used to say with a smile.

The once brightly lit streets of Kriva Gusha were now dark. The lights had been turned off years ago. The lamps, protruding from the top of numerous tall concrete posts, hung over the streets empty and rusty, their bulbs missing or smashed. During the winter, half a dozen were turned on since the nights were long and life was difficult enough for the few villagers spending the harsh winter months there. Indeed, a thick staff was a very useful commodity, almost a necessity, to help one avoid all kinds of obstacles while navigating through the dark streets, or for warding off unfriendly stray dogs. In summertime, an especially unpleasant encounter would be to come across a snake. The day before, Ivanka had almost stepped on one as it slithered along the asphalt at the side of the road.

Now, carefully proceeding along a grassy path, scouring the area in front and around it for hidden dangers, she did not see the slowly approaching mule cart loaded high with hay until it was only a few meters away from her.

"Greetings," the middle-age man walking beside the cart said grumpily while holding the bridle of the mule.

"Greetings to you, Vlado," Ivanka said. "Hay mowing in Mirna Poliana?" she continued while carefully circling around the overloaded cart.

"Uh-huh. In Mirna Poliana," Vlado replied, looking straight ahead and maintaining his measured walk in keeping with the laborious progress of the animal.

His physical appearance suggested a reserved and stern temperament, as to be expected of a former military man.

A short distance later, Ivanka shook her head. It was common knowledge throughout the village that Mirna Poliana was the bone of contention between Vlado and his cousin Grisha. The sons of two brothers had fought for years over the inheritance of their grandfather, a situation common enough now, but usually played out in a courtroom, and only very seldom as passionately contested as these two did. The old man had died clinging to his land deeds, never willing to relinquish his ownership. Their fathers had never cared, and now the two cousins had to sort it all for themselves. It turned out to be a very difficult task indeed.

The overflowing hay cart crept up the bumpy road, steadied along by Vlado. His face bore more than an expression of steely determination; he seemed greatly annoyed. What most would characterize as just an ordinary exchange of casual greetings, he regarded as nothing less than a malicious provocation and meddling. A mutter, almost a hiss came from under his breath.

"Gossipmongers," he grumbled. "Why doesn't she mind her own business? The *bitch*!"

Hot and dry, the summer was dragging on. August was at hand. It was the time of year when moonshine was on people's minds; the time to collect the wild plums for brewing brandy. In yards, along the roadsides, and in almost every neglected piece of land gone wild—places where the plum trees thrived—entire families spent hours in the pleasant activity of shaking trees and gathering the fallen fruits. This year the fruit crop was abundant and ripened early; the tree branches were breaking under the weight of their heavy yield. More plums, pears, and early apples were rotting on the ground. No longer good for eating fresh, or for jams and compotes, but some still good for making brandy.

By now, the Dimitrovs had left the village. This summer, they had gone a bit prematurely, but with good reason. Their grandson, young Nicolai, was leaving for America to attend university on a scholarship. Grandpa and Grandma had to be in the big city for his send-off. He was going to study at not just a good, but an elite establishment, and the big-city people had embraced the elitism with great gusto. A phenomenon was emerging: people who had grown up and spent most of their lives under a system that professed equality as a prerequisite for a just society were becoming obsessed with breaking free from the grip of uniformity, with climbing up and up into the elite stratum of every aspect of life—wherever it was and whatever it took to get there. The Dimitrovs were very proud of their grandson.

So they closed the shutters, locked the door and the gate, and left Kriva Gusha without ever discovering the identity of the lover-boy, or the object of his interest.

It was a morning foretelling another scorching day. It was only ten thirty and the air already hung heavy, oppressive, and still. The village was eerily quiet.

The overpowering smell of marc lingered along the streets, drifting from the barrels stacked by fences and obscured by greenery, left to ferment as far as possible from the dwellings. The rancid odor was hard to take.

Suddenly, the silence was broken by the sharp siren of an ambulance rushing through the village, drawing a few curious faces from the shady interiors of the houses to the windows. Somebody needed help; it must be serious. Also, somebody must have called. And since there were no telephones in the village, except in the mayor's office, people had to run to the only tavern in Kriva Gusha, whose proprietor owned a cellular phone. For a fee, he would let them use it. The call, of course, had to be made from the premises, and there usually were enough witnesses to spread the word later.

On this occasion, however, things acquired a much more intriguing aura when a police car was spotted closely following the ambulance. Now, *that* was unusual.

There was no permanent police force in Kriva Gusha—making the rounds, keeping the order. The place ran on autopilot, so to speak. Police came only in emergencies, when requested, or for some sort of investigation for crimes usually committed elsewhere. There were occasional break-ins and thefts in the village also, but since not a single case was ever solved, people had given up on reporting the lesser crimes. Instead, they went straight to the suspected culprits and gave them a piece of their mind.

In a few cases, the tactic worked; a small appliance and a few half-empty jars with pickled vegetables were mysteriously returned.

So this must have been an extraordinary event for ambulance *and* police to be called.

It took a couple of hours for the rumor to spread. By the time everybody had a say about the situation an incredible picture emerged: there were two dramas that had taken place in the village of Kriva Gusha. The first one had to do with the feud between the two cousins, Vlado and Grisha, which had finally come to its macabre conclusion.

Early that morning, Grisha had gone to Mirna Poliana in search of Vlado to have it out once and for all. He had his gun with him. Just like his cousin, he was a former military man with a considerably high rank. Witnesses later said that they had seen Vlado heading in the same direction with a mule-pulled cart filled with fresh manure. At some point, shots were heard and somebody called the police.

Vlado's body was found slumped against a tree near the half-empty cart. A bloody pitchfork rested nearby. There was no trace of Grisha.

Soon after the news about the drama played out in Mirna Poliana had taken over the imagination of the villagers, another rumor swept through the community. The police had been there the previous night too! They had been at Ivanka's place and had conducted a search of the house. A great amount of cash had been found, and speculation emerged about a drugs and weapons investigation going on. The police had inquired about the whereabouts of Ivanka's brother, Dragomir. Most of the villagers were startled to be reminded of the long-lost son of Kriva Gusha. Ivanka was nowhere to be found.

The blazing sun had moved far to the west, the shadows had grown long, and the oppressive heat had relented. Drifting into the pleasant warmth of the streets, out of the darkened interiors of their houses, older people slowly shuffled toward their customary places of congregation situated by one road or another. This is where they spent most of their leisure time, indulging in their most pleasant activities: chewing the fat while watching their neighbors walk by.

Today, there was plenty of fat to chew on.

A small crowd of venerable citizens of the village of Kriva Gusha had assembled around a couple of benches leaning against the whitewashed wall of a small house. Some sat and others stood, supporting themselves on homemade staffs or old, worn-out canes. Nearby, a white spotted cat and a light brown dog with a metallic spiked collar around his neck were scouring the ground looking for something to eat.

The conversation this evening was livelier than ever. The people were so absorbed in it that passersby did not get the usual attention entailing questions about their whereabouts and so forth. In fact, few seemed able just to pass by. Everybody was drawn together to hear and share news and speculation about the extraordinary events that had taken place in the last twenty-four hours. In the collective memory of the villagers, there had never been a day like this one.

Almost everyone had expressed an opinion or offered an explanation, all varying and strongly felt. But there was a consensus: all believed that the world had changed irrevocably, and it was for the worst. An observation by an elderly woman with a weather-beaten face was met by silence.

"Poor Ivanka!" she said. "It is her good-for-nothing brother who brought all this to her! Vlado was her relative also. Their grandfathers were brothers," she further reminded.

Many were already asking themselves if there was something more here than meets the eye—a thought worth exploring.

A couple of hours later, the small crowd had dwindled to a couple of elderly men in their seventies who sat next to each other, relaxed and pensive. The rest of the group had dispersed. The women had returned home to catch the latest episode of *The Bold and The Beautiful* before they got on with their evening chores. Suzy the cat and Jacky the dog, named after favorite American television characters, settled comfortably near the benches in an apparent show of trust for the old folk.

The bitter old men had seen it all. They remembered and they pondered: people used to hack each other over a piece of land, over politics, over thievery until more than half a century before, when . . . But now that was all ancient history, water under the bridge. They agreed, though, that one thing had to be acknowledged—fear brings order, while freedom breeds anarchy.

"So here is your 'freedom'! they would say." Eat it, wear it, survive it!"

It took a couple of weeks for the news to fade into the background of the all-consuming everyday life of the village of Kriva Gusha. Dragomir and Grisha were still at large, though nobody knew if they were even being looked for. The police had been very tight-lipped about both incidents. A couple of days after the fateful day, Ivanka was seen quietly going about her business. It was clear to everybody that she was in great distress.

Nobody approached her with questions, yet she knew the events that turned her life into a nightmare would not be forgotten. And if the past was to be taken into account, it was also bound that both stories would in time incorporate new elements—the suggestion of premonitions, intrigues, a curse, and further lurking mystery. A tale of conspiracy would not be out of the realm of possibility, either. After all, it would be completely in character with the usual mindset of the villagers. Unless, of course, somehow the place undergoes a complete transformation and finally catches up with the times.

But then, some things never change.

# Our Village

Each year, upon our return home to the city by the lake, as we open the front door of the house and drop our suitcases on the entrance hall floor, we both remark, "Oh my God, look at this hall! It looks so much like the one we just left a day before."

It's a reference to the living room of our house in Lyali, the village in the mountain on the other side of the ocean. Of course, we shouldn't be so surprised. We designed both of our houses, and it seems that we have been so comfortable with the first one that we have repeated the design with the second one.

Or maybe our imagination is just too limited.

There are some slight differences though. This one is a little bit larger, a little bit warmer, and a little more isolated from the outside. And the furniture is a little bit more posh. The one in the village is old, faded, and damaged by many years of use by a couple of generations. And that makes it very special indeed. In general, though, the basic pieces are the same, as well as the layout of the arrangement.

A few days would pass and we would forget about the other house and the village. We would get involved in fixing things around the house in preparation for the coming winter and the cold weather. Oh, before I forget—we like fireplaces and we have a beautiful one in our house in the village, but it runs on wood and it is not very efficient. And, of course, here we have two of them. They are much more efficient, and the one in the family room runs on gas and has a remote control, so we can turn it on and off, reducing the flames or increase them as we please, without ever getting up from the large leather sofa.

All of those things help us spend the winter months in comfort and as cheerfully as possible. Winter tends to depress us at times. We read a lot, write a lot, and regularly attend concerts. The village and our house in the mountain seldom come up in our conversations, though we like to show pictures of them to guests, especially around the holidays.

But as soon as the air gets milder, the sunshine gets brighter, and the other signs of spring become more persistent, we start noticing each other's attention span shortening. We notice one another falling into long periods of pensive silence and absentmindedness.

"Are you thinking what I am thinking?" I would inquire, and he would smile. "Lyali?"

I would persist, and he would nod.

Of course, it has been clear to me that this was the case, for I have observed the frequent visits to the hardware store to hoard the stuff he insists on carrying from here all the way back across the ocean. All the items are available now there, but this practice had acquired a ritualistic aspect, and thus it has nothing to do with practicality anymore.

A couple of months later, we would be ready and eager to head to our village in the mountains, and to the house that looks a lot like the one we spent the winter in, only a bit smaller, cooler, more open, and definitely busier. A place where people get in straight from the street with jars of homemade yogurt, bags full of vegetables straight from the garden and wild strawberries gathered from the skirts of the rocky peaks that surround the village.

◆          ◆          ◆

### The story of Vladko

The first time we saw Vladko, he was working at my cousin's house. It was during the summer. The days were long, and the temperature varied from oppressively hot at midday to sharply cool in the evening.

It was around noontime, and Vladko was standing in the shade of the house, sorting old shingles to be moved away and piled up on the other side of the road. He was in his late teens. Tall, dark, and handsome man in the making. There was something subtle and appealing about him. One might say he exuded good vibes that separated him from the rest—sort of a promise.

We inquired about who he was and was told that he was the son of the teacher. As my cousin was relating that, he kept his eyes on Vladko. There was a smile on my cousin's face. Clearly, he too liked the lad. That summer, we came to find that almost everyone in the village was charmed by this young, good-looking, special man in the making. But enough of the good stuff.

The following summer, we saw Vladko again working on a construction project. This time it was on our house. It happened sort of unexpectedly. We ran into him as we were climbing up to the upper floor, curious to see how the work on the bedroom was progressing. And there he was. It took us a while to recognize the sweet, shy Vladko in the much taller guy standing in front of a wide opening in the rough brick wall, his silhouette outlined against the bright light streaming from the outside. He must have been taking a break from work—smoking a cigarette and drinking Coke from a can. His eyes were dull, and his smile revealed a row of yellow, decaying teeth; a couple of gaping holes marking the places of a few missing ones. What had happened to the promise? Disturbed, I turned around and left him standing there, a dark shadow in the middle of a bright spot of light.

The next year, the houses were completed. There were other construction projects going on where young and old villagers were employed, but there was no Vladko to be seen on any of the sites. He had not left the village scene, but he had changed. One place he frequented at all hours of the day and during the evenings was the local pub. And this is where we saw him one night: on the outside patio, in the company of older men, at a table covered with ashtrays overflowing with squashed cigarette butts, glasses of brandy, beer bottles, and scattered empty cigarette packages among them.

Vladko had grown ever so lank, and his hair has thinned. Clearly this was not the boy we had seen just a few years earlier. Still something had remained: a disarming, appealing quality that was hard to resist, which compelled us to go sit briefly with him and exchange a few words of customary platitudes. Later, we were told that Vladko had slipped into a state of hopeless alcoholism.

The following year, when we returned to our village, Vladko was nowhere to be seen. He was gone. One cold winter night, he had gone out into the fields, caught a bad cold, and soon after passed away. It didn't take a long time for his wasted, weakened body to succumb to the bout of pneumonia. The person who told us the news about Vladko's passing away lapsed in a short pause and then smiled, and, as though to cheer us up, told us the following story:

A few months before his demise, Vladko, accompanied by a couple of his buddies, had had a lot of fun. A loud laughter and splashing noise were heard from the bottom of a gully that runs under the bridge that connects the steep, curvy road from the village with the main highway. There they were, three tipsy lads dressed up in flashy outfits, sporting pieces of extravagant lady's garb. Vladko wore a fur mantle, while one of his friends was dressed in a fancy, outmoded hat. The third wore a dazzling colorful scarf wrapped around his shoulder. All three merrily chased each other, jumping and striding energetically through the murky waters in the middle of the shallow brook, happy as larks.

It was late fall, and the fields were bare and brown—a melancholy picture except for the lively, joyous, and colorful show carried out by the bridge, in the brook, in the middle of nowhere.

As she finished the story, the villager gave a sigh and softly muttered, "We all miss him. He was such a nice young man."

◆     ◆     ◆

### The story of The Arsonist

His real name was Ilia. However, it was his nickname, given to him by the villagers that he was referred to by: The Arsonist.

One does not have to inquire for an explanation—it is evident what he had done to deserve it. However, we never bothered to ask about the details—even though we wondered about the events that lead to this unique way of branding the man.

This particular summer was the last one that we saw The Arsonist. Shortly after our departure from the village, a friend told us over the phone that there was news: The Arsonist had passed away. He was found dead somewhere in the fields surrounding the village. On the day before the discovery, he had been tending the flock of sheep and goats as usual, but at the end of the day the animals had returned home without their shepherd. His small dog was missing too.

A search was quickly organized, and at the break of dawn, The Arsonist was found lying in a meadow amongst wild flowers close by a grove of low shrubbery—his faithful dog, watching over him. A discarded, empty liquor bottle was found near his body.

It was a sad story, for sure. But what made it even more so was that he was outlived by his mother, a fragile, shriveled old woman with a pair of luminous blue eyes set wide apart under a high brow and in a youthful face starkly incongruous to her posture and gait of an old and worn out peasant. She adored her son. It was obvious. The depth of her feeling—beaming from her very soul, shining through her beautiful eyes every time she set them on her son—was a poignant example of a wondrous mother's love. To some, it was wondrous indeed, for there was hardly a single man, woman, or even a child that would bestow more than a glance at this pitiful man. And one couldn't blame them.

Only a year earlier, The Arsonist had done it again. The small house he had shared with his adoring mother had gone in flames in the dead of night, turned into cinder and smog in a matter of minutes. Mercifully, both escaped the destructive power of the inferno. In the minds of some, though, it was rather the wrong sentiment to express about The Arsonist's luck.

So when his end came, there was not much said in terms of regret and condolences. For most, the event was nothing more than the inevitable conclusion to a life that had long ago lost its purpose.

We recalled the last time that we saw The Arsonist. He was lying down on the dirt road, a step below the level of the patio in front of the local pub where he had spent the previous couple of hours drinking plum brandy all by himself. The local people were angry with him, for he had let them down. A few days earlier, he had been careless and failed to keep the flock of sheep together while tending them up the mountain, by a pine forest where wolves were known to roam. Ten sheep had veered away from the meadow and entered the woods, right under his nose, as the saying goes.

A few days later, their bare bones were found in the dense shrubbery of a thicket. Now, The Arsonist was getting his punishment. Ostracized by all, he had an entire table surrounded by empty chairs to himself while  the rest of the patrons of the establishment enjoyed themselves in merry camaraderie, laughing and drinking at the nearby tables.

After he finally emptied his last glass of brandy, he staggered outside but made it no farther than a step below the patio. As he lay there senselessly drunk with his little dog stretched out beside him, one of the men got up from his chair, stepped down, and began to kick The Arsonist's limp body.

The dog lifted his sad eyes toward the angry man and then back to his master without letting out so much as a whimper.

Nobody said anything. Most merely averted their eyes from the scene. The conversation did not seize for a moment.

Yes, this is the kind of man The Arsonist was at the end of his life.

Before I end this story, I need to mention something that, in our minds was very confusing. One summer day, we saw a handsome boy, about eleven years old, riding a bicycle along the street. His hair was blond and his eyes were blue and luminous. He was quite an impressive youngster—confident and neat. We were intrigued by him enough to inquire about his identity.

To our surprise, we were told he was The Arsonist's grandson.

"Hmm, he looks just as his grandfather," this person added.

◆           ◆           ◆

## The gypsy (a very short story)

This last summer, a familiar face confronted me on the street in a nearby town, while my better half was doing some shopping at the local supermarket.

The face belonged to a Roma person—a girl or a young woman; it was hard to say. She was pushing a baby carriage, though I can't say for sure if there was a baby in it or if the bulge I saw was just a bundle of pink blankets. She stopped a few paces ahead of me and said, "May I have a word with you?"

"No," I snapped, and continued on my way.

I recognized this shabby, worn-out creature as the pretty girl with dilated eyes, perched on wobbly stiletto shoes, who had accosted me for a few leva at this same spot a couple of years earlier. At the time, I was very obliging, and she returned to the same corner from which she came.

Later that same day, I was told that she and her stories—both the true and made-up ones—were well-known.

During that same summer she tried to stop me again. Startled, I looked at her eyes and turned away from her. She understood. Before I knew it, she leapt toward me and fixed her glare on my face—with anger bordering on madness.

"Leave me alone!" I hissed at her. "We all have problems."

I could feel the anger creeping into my eyes too. For a while, we stood there staring at each other until she finally moved away as blankness descended over her eyes.

Seeing her this last summer, I wondered if she had recognized me. And what did she have to tell me? This time her pupils were normal, but her eyes were dull and indifferent. Frankly, I was surprised to see her again.

*"Life goes on . . ."* My heart sank at the thought.

◆           ◆           ◆

## The cemetery (not much of a story)

Here we are, back in our village. Everything is the same as last year: the pristine nature, the lush ash trees that grow in leaps and bounds, taking over every little space of empty ground to the chagrin of some of the locals who are convinced that the useless, fruitless trees are sucking the oxygen from the air, suffocate people, and causing all kinds of strange ailments. Obviously, their feelings are strong enough to extend beyond the living world and the sentimental notions associated with melancholy shady cemeteries. There are only a few large trees that are allowed to grow on the boundaries of the sloping resting grounds next to the ancient small church. And that brings me to the main point of my sub-story—the latest addition to the varieties of tombstones sticking up from the ground.

There is one that strikes in most unexpected fashion: a grand monument of a young lad who was buried there sometime during our absence. It's an impressive gravestone, one that dominates the view from far away along the road that leads to the cemetery. It is a focal point which provokes—wittingly or otherwise—a sense of wonderment. We had never seen the lad, only heard a few details here and there . . . that he was shot in broad daylight in the main square of the nearby city. And that was about all.

When this occurred, there was a lot written in the press about it. But now people are reluctant to speak on the matter. And when they do, it's typically in monosyllables muttered under their breath. We have to strain our ears to hear the whisper.

Well, this will be the end of this yarn. There are many happy, heart-warming, jolly stories about our village, but for some reason, I seem to be drawn to the sad and dark ones. And this last one struck me as the darkest of them all.

# *Zorah's Cottage*

It was the last week of July, in the middle of summer. However, high up the hills, under the peak that overshadowed the village huddled below its northern skirts, the calendar seemed to matter little. It was the sun that ruled. Once it hid behind the dark, heavy clouds that brought the rains, the temperature dropped quickly. Then the water came down in torrents. The sound of continuous thunder shook the air as lightning flashes pierced the sky in rapid succession. And when the fury had finally spent itself, quiet followed. Nature was holding its breath for a while. The clouds lifted, and the peaks emerged from the darkness. Their conical outlines, separating sky from earth, obscured the horizon and dominated the village once again. The sun shone brightly from the pale blue sky, and the temperature rose. The daily rhythm of life resumed.

People who had been cooped up inside their homes for hours appeared from all directions, walking briskly while carefully avoiding the puddles left from the storm. On the outskirts of the village, a young couple, accompanied by a dog running through the wet meadow, strode among the grass, searching for something.

The chime of bells had died out, the asphalt had lost its luster, and only the trail of fresh animal droppings remained of the cows, sheep, and goats that had trotted over the pavement on their return from the pastures in the mountains. The most relaxing moment of the day was descending upon the village. The day that had started with thunder, rain, and gloom had turned into a mellow, pleasant early evening.

Suppertime was soon to be and the backyards were teeming with activity when a gray fog started to creep into the lucid air. Carried by the light breeze, first in one direction, then changing its course with the shifting wind, it kept spreading until the entire area was blanketed by its dark shadow.

It originated from a spot on the ground behind a small house—Zorah's cottage. A column of dense, white smog rose above the flames of a fire obscured by shrubbery and trees. Burning waste and grass, or simply building a cooking fire outside, especially during this time of the year, was common. Nobody paid much attention—until the white thick smog turned into a dark, foul-smelling cloud. The immediate neighbors were the first to get a whiff of it.

"What is going on? Is there a fire?" a woman ran to the street to inquire anxiously.

A man standing behind a fence seemed unperturbed.

"Oh, no, there is no fire," he casually remarked. Then he somewhat thoughtfully added: "Milena is burning Dimiter's clothes."

◆         ◆         ◆

Zorah's cottage stood at the end of the street, on the low side of it. Since the village was situated at the foothills of the mountain, its entire terrain was sloped in all directions. This meant that there was hardly a spot for a house not to have some disadvantage: the low locations were vulnerable to flooding; the high ones were too steep and exposed to the strong, cold winds that swept through during the winter months. Yet, even in these circumstances, Zorah's cottage was singled out and considered cursed for a long time on account of events that were attributed mostly to the deficiency of its location. And strangely enough, nobody could recall a time when the place had been known by any other name than Zorah's cottage.

It was named after Zorah, the girl who grew into womanhood: the one who overcame the curse by beating the odds and surviving till old age. All her siblings had failed in this, succumbing to illnesses in childhood or adolescence. Their mother had passed away at an early age a few years after giving birth to Zorah, the last of nine children. The father had not fared much better, not living long enough to see his last child pass her teens. Many of the villagers thought that all the sickness and death could be explained by the poor location of the cottage, by its lack of sunshine, and the dampness that impregnated its walls and made the air stale all year round. Many more, though, thought differently.

As a girl, Zorah was a sturdy little lass with black eyes and thick, dark-brown hair, pleated into two heavy braids that hung over her shoulders all the way down to her waist. And while everybody around her was falling into sickness—to perish sooner or later—she kept on growing strong and healthy, thriving in the darkness and dampness of the little cottage. Yet, most of the villagers considered that it was only a matter of time until she withered and faded away too. She was growing like a wild flower, with nobody to care for her, to teach her, to guide her, or to comfort her. There was no escape from her surroundings, which bred only hopelessness and helplessness. Gradually, bitterness took hold of her heart; anger and envy possessed her soul.

Life was not fair.

There was nobody to tell her otherwise. So at some point while traveling along the road to maturity, she came to an irrevocable conclusion: there was no compensation for suffering, but only fear and instincts; the fear of sickness and the will to survive ruled life.

It was the forties, and the world was at war. But the village hidden in the mountain, away from battlefields and bombs—hardly a prize for anybody to fight for—was left untouched by the events that rocked the world.

Zorah had grown into her late teens. By then, the cottage was home only to her and two of her surviving brothers. She had become somewhat of a mother to the already weakened young men, as well as the main provider for the small household. In this village, where the state of wealth or poverty was determined by the difference in ownership of only a few tens of decares***** of land, survival was the driving force in the lives of most families. To make matters worse, the land was broken into small pieces scattered all over the foothills of the mountain. It required the strength of a man to manage the work, done mainly manually and with the help of only a few domestic animals. In Zorah's household, there were no strong men to push the plow or to mind the cart. The only strong, healthy body available to take on all the chores was that of a teenage girl. And it was not enough.

Zorah became a hired hand. During the harvest, she reaped someone else's crops, dug someone else's vegetables, and gathered somebody else's fruits. Meanwhile, the few decares of land left by her father were left to go barren.

Employment was not hard to find. People sought her out for she was a good worker. She did not spare herself and gave all she had. Not because of some sense of fair exchange or integrity compelling her to keep her side of the bargain. There was no fairness in the world and she had no scruples; she had no qualms about stealing now and then. But she strained her muscles to their limits; she tested her endurance time and again to prove to herself, and everyone else, that she was strong and healthy, and that she would survive. Then she felt happy.

When she was not working in the field, she ran the household—cooking, cleaning, knitting new socks, and mending old ones. On occasion, in the summertime, she would walk along the road balancing a spade, pitchfork, or scythe on her shoulders. She would glance at the yards of the houses of the few better-off

*****    *Decare-a metric unit of area equal to 1000 square metres*

villagers. It was vacation time, and their sons and daughters, back from the cities where they attended school or university, would be sitting in the shade of a fruit tree or under a balcony, conscious of their elevated status, already acting with the aloof superiority of the intelligentsia. And the resentment that was already lodged in her chest would deepen a bit further, slowly turning into hatred.

Several years had passed since the end of the war. Great changes had occurred. An iron curtain, drawn across the middle of Europe, had divided the world. In the village under the mountain peak, somewhere east of the divide, life had been transformed too.

The cottage at the end of the street, at the low side of it, had lost two of its occupants. The men had all gone, carried away by consumption, and Zorah was the only one left there. The once small, crowded house seemed large and empty. Miraculously, Zorah continued to flourish. Her ruddy cheeks, sparkling black eyes, and shiny, thick hair left no doubt about it. It looked as though the curse had been lifted, finally. Yet, there were no young men coming to court her. The old adage, "Take a bride from sound stock," kept them away—the fear that she came from an unhealthy seed that had not produced a single offspring in a generation. Her youth and good looks, however, proved to be irresistible to Ivan, an old bachelor who lived at the other end of the village. Without much fanfare, Zorah and Ivan tied the knot and settled down to raise a family in Zorah's cottage. There was no church wedding; it simply was not done that way anymore. And that was just fine with Zorah and Ivan.

Zorah's life started to change for the better. The world may not have become fair, but justice was done, carried out by the Party. The intellectuals could argue about that, but most of the peasants living in the village under the mountain peak had no doubt whatsoever.

It did not take long for the cottage to fill up with the joyous clamor of children. Three boys were born to the new family in short intervals. The firstborn, Goran, was a dark, stocky boy endowed with his mother's eyes and hair, boisterous and willful. The second one, Dimiter, was blue-eyed and slender, with a hint of inexplicable refinement in his demeanor. Finally, a bit later, Pavel arrived—a sensitive and thoughtful boy who developed a propensity to brooding as he grew up.

Unlike their mother's childhood, theirs was free from grief, hardships, and hopelessness. They grew up roaming through the countryside, picking mushrooms and herbs, developing an appreciation of its beauty and a love for the animals. Their attachment to the village was strong; they felt secure and carefree there.

Zorah was neither a good nor bad mother. She loved her children deeply and she wanted them, above all, to be healthy. She wanted them to have everything that she had imagined all rich kids used to have when she was growing up with nothing. Since she had never known happiness, she did not believe in it, and she did not wish it for her boys. But she had seen something in the faces of the rich young men and women, sitting idle in their parents' yards, as she passed by on her way back from work in the fields. It was something she never forgot. Now she let her children do whatever they wanted and gave them everything she had, just to see them grow as confident and special as she imagined the others had been. She spoiled them and eventually lost control over them. Only their father, Ivan, could steer them into one direction or the other. Sometimes his ways of handling them were brutal.

Meanwhile, the family had to move to the city. As a stern and diligent man, Ivan fitted perfectly into the military. However, his lack of education limited his prospects. He ended up working in a depot for military supplies, while Zorah got a job in the food distribution system. Life in the city was comfortable, yet their hearts remained in the village. Every Sunday or holiday, they would jump in their new car, fill it with goods to take to the cottage, and head back home.

The small cottage had gone through renovation. Its interior was repainted, the exterior brightened by fresh whitewash, and even an extension was added to the south side facing the mountain. A couple of portable radios, a television set, and eventually a new washing machine were added to the furnishings, thus making life easier and more pleasant—especially for Zorah. The outhouse, the chicken coop, and the pigsty were still there and functioning. The pungent odor of animals, mixed with the sweet aroma of flowers growing everywhere, pervaded the air as always. Things had improved, but the place had retained its old familiarity. Moreover, now the not-so-little cottage that once stood at the end of the road was shedding its aura of isolation and loneliness. A new house was under construction and new neighbors would soon move into it.

Zorah's and Ivan's ambitions did not go very far with regard to their children's education. They had both dropped out of high school, and since it did not seem to have affected their lives adversely, the importance of education did not lie very high in their estimation. A good trade would be fine.

So Goran, Dimiter, and Pavel went as far as their own initiative and intelligence compelled them to go. Goran and Dimiter went to technical schools and Pavel, who exhibited keener inquisitiveness and brightness, graduated from high school. In hindsight, it is questionable whether that did him more harm than good. When the time came for discharging his conscript duty, his high school diploma was a factor in determining where he would serve. His background and education qualified him as most suitable for border guard service, a tough assignment that required some amount of adroitness as well as loyalty.

The three brothers grew into fine-looking young adults, and that filled their parents' hearts with pride. At least, that is how things seemed on the outside, until some of the villagers noticed that the brothers exhibited a propensity to drinking more than the norm. And that meant a lot. The mountain's inhabitants were known for their zest for the popular moonshine plum brandy that helped keep them warm during the cold weather and lifted their spirits when the isolation and monotony of village life began to weigh too heavily on their souls.

Some began to contemplate, "Maybe after skipping a generation, the bad seed had sprouted again?"

A couple more decades passed, and Zorah and Ivan had retired. Ivan had become an old man, but Zorah had a few more years to go till she would enter the last stage of life. In their retirement, they had moved back to the village permanently. The two older brothers had married and had families of their own.

Pavel's life, though, had begun to decline. The youngest of the three brothers looked older than his siblings. His haunted eyes and stony face changed his appearance permanently; even his still-young body acquired a stoop, the posture of an old man, or one who was carrying a heavy burden on his gaunt shoulders. He looked like a tormented man, silent and detached during the day while going about his business, seldom engaging in conversations, except with strangers. He spent his evenings drinking alone and listening to the radio. Even the music he preferred was foreign and alien to the villagers. He would start drinking at the end of the working day and continue through the evening, slowly falling into a stupor, drifting away into oblivion; all the thoughts and feelings that made him miserable throughout the sober hours of the day sank into his subconscious until the small hours of the night when his eyes would close under heavy lids. The empty bottle would slide from his numb fingers, and his wasted body would slumber wherever he happened to be. Pavel had become a desperate man with a secret, one he could not share with anybody—a secret that ate him up inside.

It was an old story, something that happened during his military service as a border guard. The job of a border guard was to protect the border from invaders from the outside, but most of all, from people running away from the inside. Ditches, barbed wire, and dogs were never enough. Somebody had to shoot, to stop the ones who jumped over the ditches and ran through the brightly lit neutral zones. Moreover, there was a bounty on a runaway head, just to motivate the loyal soldiers more deeply, thus ensuring that their vigilance would not fail them in a critical moment.

One dark night, in the early hours before dawn, Pavel had fulfilled his duty.

He received a reward. He was told that he had done right.

However, as time passed, as the years rolled on, the memory of that night, instead of fading away, grew in significance, slowly turning into an obsession. Maybe if Pavel's life had moved forward, if he had been less sensitive or more educated, he could have put it behind him or could have found some justification. As it happened, though, his life fell into stagnation.

He worked on odd jobs here and there, moving from one place to another, from village to village, but never far away from this place, from these mountains. Intelligent, educated just enough to start questioning, but not enough to find answers, he could not run away from himself.

Pavel's death was accidental. It happened somewhere in a place away from the village. A wrong step, a shaky ladder, and he had fallen to his death. The news did not come as a big surprise, but the event became the turning point in time that marked a spiraling downward for Zorah's family.

It had been a long time since the last Christian burial had taken place in the overgrown, unkempt cemetery next to the small, old church in the village. A padlock on the door of the church kept people out. The building had become nothing more than a picturesque relic, a reminder of a different life that existed in the not-so-distant past. The interior of the church had been stripped of its frescoes; the old icons had been taken away, and nobody knew where. At least, this was the promulgated story, though gossip abounded. Some of the tales were quite fantastic. No priest had set foot in there either. Only the bell tower had been kept in use throughout the years. The bell tolled for sad and happy occasions: one toll for the departed soul of someone local; two tolls for a relative living away; rapid melodious peals for joyous occasions, loudly proclaiming the happy event. To the outsider, the meaning of all these various sounds was quite incomprehensible.

On a gloomy, rainy day, a small procession moved along the road that led from Zorah's cottage to the cemetery. On the flatbed truck laid Pavel's body in an open, crudely made coffin. A group of women and men followed in respectful silence. Most of the women carried a variety of trays and pots filled with food, which they had prepared for the feast that would take place after the burial. Many of the men held small bouquets of flowers that grew in abundance in their yards. In front of the procession, right behind the vehicle and moving at a snail's pace, walked Zorah, Ivan, Goran, and Dimiter, followed by Liuba and Milena.

In front of the open gates of the cemetery, the truck stopped. The coffin was gingerly removed from the flatbed and brought in on the shoulders of six men and carefully laid beside a hole in the ground. The people slowly took their places around the graveside. The Secretary of the Party of the village read the eulogy. At the end of his words, all knelt on one knee and bowed their heads in a minute of silence. The coffin was covered and lowered into the ground. A wax candle was lit and left by the open grave, together with the bread and sweets left there for the departed.

The ceremony was over. Everybody moved away to a room behind the church where the food would be served. A couple of men remained at the grave to fill the gaping hole with the mound of black, sodden earth they had piled up earlier that morning.

Zorah grieved for Pavel, but it was Ivan, her husband, who took his death the hardest. The youngest and the brightest had always been his favorite. With Pavel's demise, Ivan's will to live began to weaken. A year later, he too was gone. He was an old man, and it was a natural thing that happened to him; it was only a matter of time. Zorah cried a bit, grieved a bit, and rearranged her life a bit.

Barely a year passed.

Zorah's eyes were dry. They had a blank, almost blind stare, oblivious to the world outside. Her face was drained of blood, its features distorted, frozen in a mask of sorrow and suffering.

Life had turned around again. The world was an unfair place after all.

It was the third time in as many years that she found herself in front of a funeral procession. This time, it was at the funeral of Goran—her favorite, her first-born, the one most like her. Meanwhile, more big changes had occurred in the world, but as usual, hardly any came to the village under the mountain peak. Religion was supposed to take its place in the new society, but strangely, nobody seemed to care. A funeral in the village now was no different from before. In all fairness, though, it should be mentioned that there was one significant change: the return of the crosses. After coming close to the brink of extinction, they were coming back, again adorning the old stone and the new marble headstones.

But nothing changes the way people grieve.

After their father's death, Goran and Dimiter had started to spend more and more time in the village. Liuba, Goran's wife, had remained in the city. Suddenly, the energetic, enterprising, efficient factory worker had found that she had the talent and initiative of a businesswoman. She began by selling baby shoes and T-shirts in a stall in the market, and she had ended as the proprietor of a couple of small stores that sold children's clothes. A bright future was beckoning to her. During all that transformation, Goran was not at her side, sharing in her new life. The better she did, the worse he felt. So he left his wife and moved to the village permanently, drowning his disappointments and sorrows in drink.

Liuba drove from the city for the funeral of her husband in her newly purchased, second-hand Western car. A couple of hours later, she left. The business could not wait. She generously paid all expenses, and as soon as she reached the outskirts of the city, she stopped at a place specializing in burial monuments to order a marble tombstone.

A few weeks later, the elaborate, almost extravagant, marble pieces were brought and mounted on a concrete foundation that was poured over the still unsettled earth of the grave. A large cross was erected over the massive structure. A couple of days later, Liuba showed up in the village and went straight to the cemetery to inspect how the work had been done. Satisfied with what she saw, she drove back.

Back in her cottage, Zorah spent her days sitting and staring at the picture of trees, grass, and flowers outlined by the window frame against the backdrop of the rocky mountain peak. Her mind drifted, and her body was limp. Only her lips moved from time to time, letting out a moan: "Oh, Goran, Goran! Where are you?"

Goran was always on her mind.

In a short time, some aspects of her appearance, as well as of her behavior, changed. She hung a small cross on her neck, and she began to show an openness that was almost alien to her nature. She began to recall her long-deceased brothers and sisters, her father, even began making references to her mother, whose face she couldn't even remember, having lost her such a long time ago.

More poignantly, her bitterness had been drained of all its potency; she could no longer draw any strength from it. Maybe there was more to life then what she thought? Maybe, after all, it was not only people who made life flow in one direction or other.

Zorah was growing old. She had a lot to ponder, and the time to do it was now. She started having doubts and fears. The small cross hanging about her neck was a small reassurance, a way to ward off the bad things happening to her and hers. At least it would not do any harm. It seemed as though Zorah's life was approaching its end.

A couple of years earlier, Dimiter and his wife, Milena, had left their home in the city and moved in with Zorah. Now they were by her side, but it made no difference. She had bore three sons, but the one she cared most about, the strongest and the most similar to her, had left her forever. The quiet Dimiter and his fragile-looking wife were of little solace to her. To Zorah, they brought only disappointment. Understanding and compassion for the weak were feelings she had never known.

It was the fall of Ivan's death. Autumn was descending upon the mountain. The bare ground was changing into a pastel brown, and the birch forest was turning light green with splashes of yellow and light orange. Only the pine trees stood out against the dull hues of the gray, rocky hills. The village was falling into a melancholy silence. Its streets had been deserted by the children who invaded the place during their summer vacations and had now returned to the cities. A sense of loneliness and desolation enveloped the village in a claustrophobic embrace.

Feelings of hopelessness and despondency were strangling Milena's heart. There had never been a true closeness between her and her husband, but now, the estrangement that took years to drive an impervious wedge between them had become complete. Both were in need of a shoulder to lean on. They had lived for years in the shadow of Zorah, Ivan, and the rest, and after Ivan's death, life looked even gloomier to Milena.

It was just an ordinary fall day, a bit on the cool side, with the sun peeking out from behind fluffy, white clouds drifting across the sky. Milena was nowhere to be found. Nobody knew where she could have gone. The previous evening, Dimiter had left her in the cottage and gone to the village pub, just the same as he had done every evening, all year round. He was back, as usual, in the dead of night, staggering into the room and dropping onto the bed in a drunken stupor. The next morning, when Zorah inquired about Milena's whereabouts, he was taken by complete surprise. He could not recall anything.

Milena was found lying on the floor of the empty, cold church. The bare walls, the empty altar, the dust and the silence, the ambiance of neglect and destruction— all were unbearable. But what oppressed and chased away some made it the right place for others, those burdened by life and desperate to escape this world.

Milena had come here to die. Where most saw emptiness, she saw salvation.

Apparently, her time had not yet come. She was unconscious but still breathing. An ambulance was called, and she was taken to a nearby hospital where her stomach was pumped, emptied of the poison she had swallowed. She was revived and left to spend some time under observation. A few days later, she was released from the hospital and returned home. Now, on top of all the misery she had felt before, was added the humiliation of exposing the depth of her despair and her inability to face life.

In Zorah's eyes, Milena sank to even greater depths.

She dismissed the incident with a few words: "What is wrong with her? She has a fine husband—no worse than the rest. What else does she want?"

And now she was left with them only.

She felt so lonely.

The small village under the peak was changing slowly but surely. For some, the changes were coming too slowly, for others they were happening too fast.

To Zorah, nothing mattered anymore. During the summer, she spent her days soaking up the warmth of the hot mountain sun. During the winter, she kept herself busy inside the cottage, with the television and radio to distract her.

In the spring, after her ordeal, Milena went to the city for a while. The small apartment on the outskirts of the city was neat and quiet. For a few days, she stayed cooped up inside, busying herself with whatever housework she could find, her mind free to wander. Since the night she almost died, she had actually been growing. She was slowly formulating a new perception of the world. She was not strong enough, but she was willing to try. The first step for her was to get out of the village, away from her husband who had stopped paying any attention to her, and away from Zorah, whose strength was crushing her. Away from the small cottage dominated by its keeper.

So Milena never went back. She found a job. She forged some new friendships and renewed some old ones. She had not found happiness, but she had found reasons to live.

Dimiter came to visit her a few times, but never stayed for long. The only place he felt at home was at the village. Meanwhile, he was growing ever so gaunt. His blue eyes had clouded, and his delicate face had lost its character. He spent every evening drinking in the village pub, and every night he would stagger along the road, advancing to his mother's cottage like a leaf blown by the wind. Regularly, he asked his mother for money and she never refused, even though she was hardly able to manage on her pension.

Life went on for Zorah and Dimiter, mother and son, together yet each alone in their own world. Every passing year, the village went through a renewal: new, whitewashed, red-roofed houses would spring up in the hills; old ones were renovated. Meanwhile, Zorah's cottage grew shabbier and messier. Neglect was taking its toll. Like the house itself, its inhabitants' appearances became seedy and piteous.

Zorah's life came to an end quietly in her bed, like a candle that had burned out without sputtering and flickering. It happened in the early dawn while Dimiter was sleeping off his drunkenness from the night before. A few months later, Dimiter followed her.

The cause: who knows? The doctors who performed the post-mortem put down some diseases with fancy names, but the people in the village knew it was drunkenness that killed him, just as it had his brothers.

Many years had passed since the time people here believed in curses. There had been progress in the world, and it reverberated even in this place. A testament to this could be seen in the satellite dishes sticking from the roofs of the houses, in the variety of foreign music that could be heard blasting from the radios, obscuring the sounds of chiming bells, barking dogs, and crowing roosters. But if it was not a curse, where did this sickness of the soul come from? For it was not physical decline but something else that came from deep inside them that killed Zorah's sons.

◆          ◆          ◆

The burning went on for several days. During the day, Milena would be seen going in and out of the cottage, busily washing and cleaning, putting the place in order. The first thing she would do in the morning was to open the windows wide, start the fire outside in the yard, and place a large pot on it to heat water for the washing. The clothesline stretched across the small yard would be covered all day with a row of freshly washed drying sheets, blankets, towels, and wall hangings, while Milena—stooped over a pot of hot water—kept on scrubbing pots, pans, and every imaginable gadget that she had found in long-unopened drawers. Her movements were measured, and her absorption in her work was thorough. The expression on her face was of a quiet half-smile.

The cottage's front door would be left open all day long. People passing by threw quick glances in at her; some even greeted her, and she returned their greetings with the same unperturbed serenity that radiated from her whole being. Others entered the small yard. She approached them and talked to them with a kind of confidence and dignity that made them leave her with a sense of respect they had never felt before toward this small, fragile woman.

At the end of the day, before the sun set behind the mountains, she would go behind the house and start a new pit fire over the cinder that marked the spot she had it lit the night before. And a new stack of clothes would go into the new pyre to be devoured by the red blazing flames.

The cleaning and airing lasted a few days. Then the painting started. The fence metal gate, the front door, and the window frames all got a new coat of shiny green paint. The outside wall that faced the street was whitewashed. Finally, flowers potted in tin cans were placed outside on the window sills.

When all the work was finished—pots and pans scrubbed; sheets and covers washed, dried, and put away; every corner inside aired; all the clothes burned and their ashes scattered by the wind—Milena closed the windows, locked the front door of the house and the one outside, and headed toward the village square to catch the bus for the city, carrying only a purse in her hand.

Before she made the turn at the junction between the street and the main road, she stopped to throw a brief glance back over her shoulder at the cottage—her cottage. First, she glanced at the blue, clear sky and smiled. Then she lowered her eyes and fixed her stare at the pretty, cheerful-looking house with its whitewashed walls, now bathed in bright sunshine. Finally, she let her gaze linger over the rows of pink and red geraniums lined along the windows sills, trembling on their long green stems, swaying in the light breeze.

For a few moments she stood there, taking in the scene. Then she turned, squared her shoulders, and, looking straight ahead, strode toward the bus stop.

# The Concert

A couple of days had elapsed since Nina and Ivo had quarreled. Although, in retrospect, the argument seemed as just a silly, overblown reaction to an insignificant disagreement, it looked as the cooling-off period was going to last for a while.

Maybe this was due to a number of aggravating circumstances: the roof was leaking; their son had moved away and seldom called, if at all. Even the upcoming Easter, usually an uplifting occasion, appeared to have a detrimental effect on their moods.

In the afternoon, Nina had felt particularly gloomy. A drive around the city, alone with her simmering anger, seemed like a good idea. So she put on her coat, picked up her purse, and left the house. On the way out she caught a glimpse of Ivo sitting in an armchair reading a magazine.

Oblivious to the passing of time and with no destination in mind, she kept cruising aimlessly along the streets listening to the car radio. Before long, the music touched her in a particular way. Her anger subsided as she immersed herself into remembrances of happier times.

She remembered the Easters of her childhood—the most joyous of all holidays. She recalled her son growing up and the Easters she had tried to make for him as memorable and happy as they had been for her. She had done her best.

Now it all seemed pointless.

By the end of her ride, Nina's agitation had mellowed, but her sadness had deepened.

Back home, she saw Ivo sitting in front of the television set watching the screen with a petulant expression across his face. She also noticed the couple of concert tickets lying on the small table in the entrance hall. Next to them was placed the exact fare for parking. It was the usual reminder of a forthcoming concert from their seasonal subscription. Ivo must have remembered tonight's performance and had left the tickets and the fare there, as usual.

It was time to head for the concert hall. For a few minutes, Nina lingered by the front door in a fruitless wait for her husband to join her. As her patience started to wear thin, she went looking for him.

"Time to leave," she said, annoyance creeping in her voice as she observed his relaxed posture, which was unchanged from an hour before.

"I am not coming," he said laconically.

"Then, why did you place the tickets on the table?" Nina inquired. "You even have the fare for the parking ready," she added quickly.

"I am not coming," he reiterated stubbornly.

During the entire exchange, Ivo stared straight ahead at the TV, without sending so much as a glance in Nina's direction.

"Well, suit yourself," she snapped.

Then she energetically turned on her heels, crossed the entrance hall, and slammed the door.

The traffic was light; the trip to the concert hall was a short one.

In the lobby, only a small crowd of people milled about, circling one way, then the other. Nina retreated to a secluded corner by the windows to wait till the doors to the auditorium would open and she could take her usual seat. The hall had been refurbished recently, and it looked and smelled like new. She was glad that she came.

Inside, the musicians had already occupied the stage and were busily checking their instruments while occasionally glancing at the crowd that was now drifting in. The concertmaster entered, took a bow, and gave the cue to the orchestra to tune in. The conductor and the solo performer followed, greeted with polite applause. The first notes of the first piece on the program—Gustav Mahler's *Songs from Das Knaben Wunderhorn*—resounded through the hall now cloaked in the dim light emanating from a constellation of pot lights installed in a canopy hanging from the ceiling. A rich baritone voice blended beautifully with the music, rising powerfully above the orchestra at times. Nina's heart swelled with tenderness, love, sadness, and melancholy.

The first part of the concert was over quickly. An exodus ensued to the foyer, to the refreshment bars, and to the music store. Nina remained seated, scanning the newly mounted wooden panels along the walls and the recently extended stage now empty but for the grand piano pushed into a corner.

Twenty minutes later, the musicians were back behind their music stands and the people were back in their seats. The conductor motioned with his baton and the sound of the Fifth Symphony by Tchaikovsky descended upon the hushed audience. Nina closed her eyes as pictures from the past rushed into her head and memories started rolling through her mind. The empty chair next to her bothered her no more.

And from the depths of her mind, long forgotten events and images transported her to the past, to another world—to a reality glossed over by promises of an unattainable perfect future while struggling in a hopeless present. From the dreary and prosaic place of her youth, a soothing recollection emerged.

She remembered Sava.

◆         ◆         ◆

A thin pile of papers filled with her slanted handwriting lay on the table: the essays expounding on three topics, as well as the solutions of the accompanying problems. It was the final exam on a difficult subject.

Less than an hour earlier, she had encountered Sava emerging from the examination room. He was shaking with agitation, and his forehead glistening with perspiration.

"Darn it! I flunked!" he blurted. Facing Nina, caustically he had snapped at her, "Let's see how *you'll* do!"

Nina had tried to dismiss his remark. Still, the implied challenge had unnerved her some. She felt a faint flutter in her stomach.

"Next," the professor said, looking at her expectantly.

Hastily, Nina collected her papers, crossed the room, and took the vacant seat beside him.

All seemed to be going well at the start. The professor read the papers and checked the solutions of the problems meticulously. He seemed satisfied.

"Well . . . good. Now let me walk you through the rest of the material. I have a few questions."

The first question stumped her. The professor was disappointed.

"Let us continue with this topic," he persisted further.

Quickly, things went from bad to worse.

The professor's voice grew sharper, even sarcastic. Nina's head was spinning.

Outside the building, Sava was waiting.

"You flunked too, didn't you?" he said.

"I was close to passing though!" she replied adamantly.

"Ugh. Really?"

Sava was smiling.

In a state of high excitement bordering on bravado, they had rushed to the closest restaurant located on the edge of a nearby park. Immediately they ordered a bottle of red wine. Before the food was served, the bottle was emptied and half a pack of cigarettes had gone up in smoke. Both felt giddy. By the time they left the place, it was late evening.

Outside the noisy, smoke-filled restaurant, the velvet touch of warm air heavy with the scent of fresh greenery gently brushed against their faces. The mellow summer night had transformed the lonely park into a cozy, intimate garden under a starry sky. A seductive feel of timeless serenity pervaded all. Enthralled, Nina and Sava dropped onto an empty wooden bench along the pathway. He had his arm around her shoulders; she leaned against him.

He kissed her lightly.

"You're tipsy," he said. "I like you that way."

After a long pause, he continued. "How about you and me going steady?"

*What a silly thing to say!* Nina thought. Both were already going steady—with someone else.

"All right," she replied.

They kissed some more.

The next day, Nina slept in. It was midday when she made it to the university. Sava was already there, sitting on the concrete steps in front of the building, all by himself. She joined him. For a long while they sat in silence, soaking up the warm sun, contemplating. Finally, he spoke.

"It's over, isn't it? You've changed your mind."

"Yes."

Another long pause followed.

"Let's go to the café," he said.

"All right," she agreed meekly.

The café was rather splendid. The furniture was opulent—massive wooden tables with marble tops, deep armchairs upholstered in red plush cloth, lace curtains covering huge windows that overlooked the street, crystal chandeliers hanging from high, ornate ceilings. The air, permeated with the pervasive smell of cigarettes, was stale and heavy. The pungency never went away, even in the summertime when the breeze blew inside, billowing the curtains across the wide-open windows. The menu was simple and limited: there were no fancy desserts and most of the time not even coffee to be served. Its customers spent hours over a glass of inexpensive cognac, vermouth and soda water. The waitress knew all the regulars and as soon as she spotted them coming through the door she would inquire loudly, "The usual?"

Invariably, the answer was affirmative.

Nina and Sava had the usual also: a glass of cognac and soda water. Sava was in a ponderous mood.

"I have a proposition for you," he said, taking a sip from the dark yellow liquid before he continued.

"Let's make a pact. If both of us are still single at twenty-eight, let's get married. We get along well. We like each other."

"Yes," Nina said sincerely. "That's a *great* idea."

"Promise?"

"Promise!"

Both seemed very enthusiastic and deadly serious—at least for the moment.

Sava's steady girlfriend, Mila, was petite, pretty, and fickle. Before long, Mila broke it off with him—she had found a new boyfriend. Her new interest's most-attractive attribute was his car, a Moscvich. Scorned for a car!

Sava was devastated. In his way of thinking, though, it was not his cheating sweetheart who had betrayed him, but life itself. So Sava directed all his anger at the car, developing an obsession against the boxy, sturdy, clumsy-looking vehicle. And he took his revenge, vandalizing every Moscvich he could lay his hands on. In the cover of darkness, on an empty street, wherever he happened to come across a Moscvich, he would pull off a mirror, a windshield wiper, a hubcap, or let the air out of a tire—anything that struck his fancy. He would hoard the vandalized loot—his trophies—in his rented room and show them occasionally to Nina, to demonstrate how successful he had been. Nina was worried.

"Aren't you afraid?" she asked. "They'll catch you and you'll get it real bad."

"I know how to get out of it. Look! It's brilliant."

Sava pulled out his internal passport and spread it open. Neatly fitted between its pages was a photograph of Yuri Gagarin—his smiling eyes looking straight back at Nina.

"What does Gagarin have to do with all this?" Nina asked, puzzled.

"Everything! I already tested my theory."

And he proceeded telling her a story to illustrate his point. A militiaman had surprised him while he was hanging around a Moscvich parked on a side street in the middle of the night. The militiaman's suspicions had been aroused, so he had asked Sava to produce his internal passport. Sava had done so. The militiaman had opened it and he had seen Gagarin's picture. Immediately, he closed the document and handed it back to Sava.

"You carry a photo of a great hero in your passport. Commendable, comrade!" he said, and walked away satisfied.

"Impressive!" Nina said.

Around that time, Sava's drinking was getting out of hand. On occasion, Nina would wake up in the late hours of the night to a persistent whistle. She would get up and take a look at the street from the window, just to reassure herself of what she already knew: it was Sava. Then she will throw a raincoat over her pajamas and step outside. He would be standing there, swaying on the sidewalk, waiting,

"I'm pissed," he would say. "I'm a bit confused. Would you take me home?"

She would shove her arm under his to steady him, then start pushing and guiding him, slowly walking toward his apartment only a couple of blocks up the street. In front of the building, she would let go of his arm.

"Here, we're at your place," she would say. "Now you go up by yourself."

He never heeded her words. Instead, he would take a look around, then grab her by the shoulder.

"Thank you," he would say. "But I can't let you walk back alone, in the middle of the night. I am a gentleman."

She did not argue; she expected it. At the end of the short trip, Sava would kiss Nina's hand while executing a slight and unsteady bow. Then, he would wait for her to enter her house and only after the door closed behind her would he turn and start walking back to his place. She would rush upstairs to stand by the window, her eyes fixed on his broad back accentuated by the raincoat's belt tied around his waist. He would stagger away; his silhouette slowly dissipating into the darkness.

Indeed, Sava was brought up to be a gentleman. He was born into wealth, had been cared for by a governess, and was surrounded with all the material comforts his privileged situation could afford—until all was taken away. From that time on, he was left to grow up with the bitterness of what he could have been. He could never forget that. It had made him hard and arrogant. He never missed an occasion to demonstrate his good breeding and show his contempt for the usurpers.

Nina and Sava had a lot in common: both were romantic; both believed in true love and friendship and in old-fashioned values. Also, both felt alienated and doomed. They would often lament that they were born too late and did not belong to these times. Neither spoke about the future.

At times they played games, pretending to be living in a different, gentler, and brighter time.

The Old Russian Club was one of the city's renowned restaurants. It was more expensive than the rest and therefore it was also exclusive—unaffordable for most. Its appeal was derived from its premises. The Club was located in an old house, remodeled to suit its new purpose. An adjacent garden surrounded by a high wall hid it from the street and provided charming intimacy. During the summertime, on certain days of the week, there would be live music—a couple of musicians playing from a balcony overlooking the garden. The menu was mundane, but the tartar steak and "Pavlova's Dessert" were fabled. Reservations were required.

It was a truly memorable evening when Sava invited Nina to The Old Russian Club. Naturally, it was supposed to be an old-fashioned, elegant dining fantasy, which meant that sharing expenses was out of the question. Dressed in their freshly brushed and pressed everyday garb, and carefully groomed—Sava sporting a gold watch, ring, and cigarette lighter—they arrived, determined to have a great time. Clutching a bouquet of flowers in his hand, he had walked the two blocks from his place to pick up Nina, refusing to let her come by his place and collect him—a more sensible option, considering it was on her way. But Sava was sticking to the script.

Sitting opposite each other, never taking their eyes off one another, and playing the consummate couple in love, they felt on top of the world. The attention they drew from people who occupied nearby tables added a piquant edge to their sharpened awareness. It was a wonderful life—the life that could have been.

◆          ◆          ◆

The music from the orchestra was flowing. It was powerful, sad, tender, dreamy—the kind of music played in The Old Russian Club. But this was now. She had been transported for a while to a different place, to a time long ago that had come back almost alive, like in the movies. It was a bit confusing. Nina's dreams had come true. Not exactly the way they had imagined it with Sava, but how could they have imagined a life so different than theirs?

A while before she left, Sava got married. Both had graduated and were on their way to building their careers. They had remained friends, but their contact was occasional—not what it used to be.

One Sunday afternoon, Sava had showed up at Nina's place unexpectedly. As she opened the front door, she was surprised to see him standing on the platform of the staircase, a bottle of brandy in his hand.

"Hello," he said. "May I come in? I have something to tell you."

He looked a bit flustered.

Inside the apartment, he immediately dropped into one of the armchairs. Nina stood by with an expectant look in her eyes.

"Mila wants me back," he said. "Her boyfriend caught her cheating on him with some bum and dropped her. No Moscvich, no boyfriend. She came back to me."

Sava was musing: "What should I do?"

Nina was preoccupied with her own problems and plans for the future.

"You know best. Do you love her?" she asked automatically.

"No."

She glanced at the bottle he had left on the small table next to the armchair.

"Hmm," Nina said. "What's the bottle for?"

Sava did not seem to be listening.

"Thought you'd be more helpful," he said without reproach. "How are things with you?"

"Nothing special."

Nina was evasive.

Four months after that, Sava had married and shortly afterward, Nina left the country.

It was the beginning of the nineties when Nina and Ivo embarked on a journey to the old country. Things had changed there and they were going to see for themselves. On the way, they had decided to stop over in Italy to visit an old classmate of Nina's.

It was a happy reunion filled with endless chats and reminiscences. However, on one occasion, the conversation took an unexpected turn.

"Any plans to meet some old friends?" the former classmate inquired casually.

"Not really," she replied, pausing for a moment. "Actually, I *would* like to find an old colleague from university." Then remembering something, she continued, "He married a girl who attended your university—Mila—a pharmacy major."

"You mean Sava?" There was more than surprise in her friend's voice.

"You know Sava?" Nina blurted, her excitement growing.

Her old classmate had plunged into uneasy silence.

"Sava passed away. A couple of years ago," she finally muttered. "Brain tumor . . . after Chernobyl."

It took a long time for Nina to shake off the stupor; for her eyes to lose the blank look they had acquired and to fill with tears of sadness. It had never occurred to her that the trip back would be anything but joyous; never considered that the merciless march of life had gone on there the same as anywhere else; never imagined that the world she left behind long ago was no more.

Nina never cried for Sava again after that. From time to time, though, she would remember him, and on occasion—as this evening—she would miss him.

◆          ◆          ◆

The lights came on. The thunderous end of Tchaikovsky's Fifth Symphony was followed by an enthusiastic burst of applause. The crowd stood. Some kept on clapping as most started to leave the hall.

Nina crossed the glass foyer and took the elevator down to the underground garage. There, she got into her shiny, beautiful car and joined the slow-moving procession of many shiny, beautiful cars.

The car crept up the steep ramp until it reached the brightly-lit street flooded by hordes of people exiting the theater located opposite the concert hall. For a moment, she felt exhilarated, and the ridiculous thought that maybe she was born too early flashed through her mind only to be rejected instantly. Presently, she made a left turn, leaving behind all the glitz, entering a wide, stately boulevard. The traffic was light, with only a few cars passing in both directions.

The anger, the sadness, and the anguish had abated. She had regained her equilibrium and felt reassured. It had been a lovely concert.

A very long day was coming to an end.

# *Retrospect*

Each of us is alone on the heart of the earth
pierced by a ray of sun:
and suddenly it's evening.

Човек е сам върху сърцето на земята
Пронизан от един единчък слънчев лъч
И неусетно пада вечерта.

Salvatore Quasimodo

It is a calm, rainy day. Thick, heavy mist hangs over the flanks of the peak and the mountains, spread out to both sides of it like a white shroud suspended from the sky. Underneath it, the air is translucent, fresh, and mild, in pleasant contrast to the usual sharpness that sets in as soon as the sun disappears below the horizon. The rainfall is steady and monotonous. Besides the muted hiss of drops landing gently on leaves of trees and bushes, there is no other sound to disturb the perfect quiet. It is peaceful and pristinely beautiful; sense of serenity so profound, it makes one think of eternity.

I am sitting outside on the verandah covered by cement slabs, under the jutted balcony of the floor above. The dry concrete around me is light gray, almost white. Beyond the sharp line separating the protected from the exposed area, the wet surface of the slabs had acquired a dark charcoal, almost black color. I am going to sit here forever, I think—or at least as long as the rain keeps coming down. Nothing can disturb me now. Nothing.

Today there will be no need to water the newly planted flowers in the cemetery, either. Lately I have been going there frequently—some days more than once.

So far, it has been a very strange summer, not like any other since we started spending them here. Each trip back, till this one, had been bittersweet, carefully choreographed in an attempt to capture only the good memories, and to avoid any circumstances that could bring back any of the bad ones, blocked out of my mind, stored in my sub-consciousness. That is, until about a month ago, when I was startled by a most unexpected phone call.

Not many people have the number of my cell phone, and those who do seldom call. Wireless communications are expensive here. The voice was strange and it took me a while to realize that this was a man I used to know many years before, one who I hadn't seen for ages. Exactly the kind of person I have been avoiding.

As it turned out, the conversation that ensued was quite pleasant. He had kept in touch with friends and had a lot of news to share, most of which was sad. The good news usually doesn't travel as fast, nor is remembered for as long.

We couldn't meet, but we promised to make an effort to see each other sometime in the future. I experienced a strange sense of elation; it seems I have put much behind already. The past had lost its grip on my soul. And then, ten days ago, it all changed. Aunt Dora had been buried and there was nobody left to remind me of bygones anymore.

So I have come here, to the village of my maternal ancestors, to spend some time in respite before the final good-byes, to enjoy myself. For this actually is just a happy ending of a long story. Besides, it is the right place for the end of a journey. The past here was put to rest, buried long ago. Now to fill the empty hours, I vainly search the tombstones in the shady cemetery next to the old, small church for names of people I have only heard of and did not know, for people with whom I share the same bloodline with—a tangible connection to this land.

Tomorrow I am leaving. But before I head to the airport, I am going to Aunt Dora's place to pick up the picture. It is her bequest to me. Indeed, it is more than I expected.

◆          ◆          ◆

There is nothing I would like more than sit under the large round table and play with the set of pink toy furniture. First, I would arrange them carefully, then drop, one by one, set of bombs dangling from hooks attached to the wings of a toy airplane that I circle over the pink chairs, tables, and baby carriage before releasing the destructive cargo upon.

The crisp, white tablecloth hanging around me provides seclusion and intimacy—a place of my own. Grandpa's legs, dressed in trousers made of fine cloth, matching socks, and a pair of shiny shoes, are a reassuring presence rather than an intrusion. It is quiet. Occasionally a pair of feet clad in colorful knitted socks appears next to the table and move away with small steps. They belong to the maid, who brings grandpa's omelet, fruit, and finally, nuts, which he starts cracking with predictable regularity. The midday meal is almost over, though, for me, the best part is just beginning. A sequel of motions performed with ritualistic precision follows every second nut-crack: Grandpa's hand appears under the table proffering a nut, which I take and shove in my mouth immediately. This also is done in silence.

Before long, the cracking noises stop. Grandpa pushes his chair back and walks away from the table. The pair of legs clad in colorful knitted socks appears again, and I know for certain that it will not be long before the white, draped tablecloth will be removed. Quickly I crawl out of the soon-to-be-exposed hideout and run to the adjacent room where Grandpa has already deposited himself on the green Viennese loveseat—absorbed in the news reports flowing from the radio. The radio is placed on a round crochet cover atop a round table situated in the middle of the room.

I jump next to him and comfortably wiggle under his shoulder in anticipation of the tap on my head that invariably follows. With hands folded in my lap, I wait patiently for the moment the news is over and our conversation can begin. The news is all about the war, which is still far away and still somebody else's problem, though its ominous rumble continues to creep slowly eastward. Its inevitability: hard to deny.

All the while, my eyes remain fixed on a picture hanging on the wall opposite me. It shows a large terrace overlooking the sea. The floor is covered in marble. Far to the left and to the right, respectively, are visible a couple of columns topped with Ionic capitals. Facing the sea is a group of men dressed in white togas and women wearing simple, elegant sheaths that hug their bodies. Their hair is piled up in elaborate coiffures and their feet are clad in open sandals tied with strings that run up their ankles.

The place, the people, and their clothes are all strange. The picture beckons to me and fills me with wonderment.

I watch it with fascination.

◆          ◆          ◆

I am no longer a little girl. I am a sad, grown-up woman trying to find happiness in a sad world. Perched on a high stool by the counter in a nightclub in a new, fashionable Black Sea resort, I stare off into space, numb with hopelessness, just passing time. The sun has bleached my light-brown hair, which I have pulled tight around my head into a ponytail. It frames my tanned face in a golden glow. I am wearing a yellow muslin dress with white polka dots that fits tightly about my small, firm breasts and thin waistline. The skirt over the voluminous petticoat billows over my crossed legs, which are clad in white high-heel shoes. The right one rests on the crossbar of the stool, the left one crosses over the right. My hands are occupied with a cigarette holder in the left one and a glass of cognac in the right one.

I am all alone in a room full of people, acutely self-conscious of the glances of men standing behind me or sitting next to me. They are natives, just like me, who are flocking into the new summer resorts in search of foreign girls—adventure-seekers hoping for more than just a night of pleasure or even a short, forgettable affair. They are what we call "glarusi."

I feel a whiff of warm breath on my cheek. I turn around. My eyes meet the dark gaze of a local man. I am absolutely sure of it, though it is clear to me that he is mistaken at guessing my nationality. He whispers in my ear something in German while his arm slides around my waist.

"Sorry, I don't understand," I whisper back with a measure of genuine regret in the native language we both know. His attractive facial features lose their attractiveness when hardened by mild shock and considerably higher annoyance. Without a word, he hastily pulls his arm from my waist, swiftly turns, and disappears into the crowd.

Again I am alone, wondering why I came here in the first place.

*What am I looking for?*

Back in the hotel, I kick the high-heeled shoes off my feet and drag a chair from the room to the small balcony. I raise my feet and place them on the cool metallic railings, pushing back the chair until I feel comfortable, and then fix my gaze at the sea panorama in front of me. The black mass of restless waters gently breaking in waves at the shoreline shines, illuminated by the moonlight. Its rhythmic rumble is soft and soothing.

I could sit here, listening, watching with fascination forever. It vaguely reminds me of a picture I have seen before.

◆          ◆          ◆

A few years later.

I am boarding the U-ban at Alexander Plaza. The cold sweat on my palms, the wild racing of my heart in my chest, and the dryness of my lips won't go away. It is not only the border crossing that brings on the anxiety attack—it is all those soldiers standing on the platform with machine guns in their arms, their watchful eyes leveled at the people below. It all makes me feel woozy.

The train is going to take me to the Zoo in the West zone, on the other side of an impenetrable divide. The train passes by abandoned, dilapidated buildings on the East side. I keep my eyes glued to the window as though trying to imprint the desolate picture in my mind forever, since I am never going to see it again.

Finally, the train stops and I disembark. I've made it, and there is no going back. I am in West Berlin in the springtime, just before Easter. The streets are crowded with people, and the store windows are dazzling: decorated with chocolate candies wrapped in sparkling, shiny foil, and chocolate-covered pastries, surrounded by or nestled in a canopy of paper garlands and flowers in bright, fresh, spring colors. Inside, the air is impregnated with the smell of sweets, perfume, and makeup fragrances. Everywhere I look I see Plenty, Orderly, Vibrant. I am scared, confused, and dizzy with worry. I am all alone. I have made it. Now what?

◆          ◆          ◆

The plane slowly ascends over the city, looping over the downtown area before reaching the blue waters of the lake. The slew of sailing boats dotting the view grows ever so distant.

This is my home city on the other side of the ocean. It's one of the most beautiful places in the world, as far as I am concerned, and this great lake, one of many in this region, is one of the friendliest and prettiest water vistas anywhere. It's not a sea, but nevertheless just as vast and impressive in its own way.

Soon the plane sets its northeast course, piercing the fluffy white blanket of clouds that obscures the earth below.

I am on my way to what used to be home once, a long time ago.

Much time had elapsed since Grandpa has passed away, and in the last few years I have been getting news of aunts and uncles joining him. The next generation—the one I belong to—is slowly aging, busy with the joys and disappointments of their lives and their children's lives. They do not concern me. It would be fair to mention that they never really cared about me, and, in return, neither did I for them.

The only one left from the previous generation is Aunt Dora.

Aunt Dora never married. She lives in one of the rooms of the old house surrounded by objects and old furniture that I remember from my childhood. The rest of the large house is inhabited by people who had moved there long ago. Only the radio is gone, replaced by a much more modern version that now sits on the same old table, over the same old crochet cover that has since acquired a deeper yellowish hue. Everything looks worn out, damaged by the soot from the coal-burning stoves.

My eyes linger over the furnishings, walls, drapes, and the carpet covering the wooden floor. And in spite of all its grayness I feel comfortable and reassured somehow.

Suddenly, my eyes stray into one of the walls, toward the spot where the picture used to be. It is still there. I am overwhelmed by surprise—at myself. Gone is the fascination, the yearning; the picture has lost its pull on me. Now all I see is a quaint print, surrounded by a wide, yellowish mat and a black-lacquered wooden frame. There is nothing intriguing or spellbinding there anymore to draw my attention to it for longer than just a perfunctory look. Still, I would like to have it, for past's sake. I would like to hang it on one of the walls in my house in the city by the lake. The dreams are gone, but the past remains—at least for a little while longer.

The doorbell rings, and my husband rushes to open the front door. I look back and see that he had disappeared—probably stepped outside—and closed the door behind him. I am curious, but not enough to go see what is going on.

Within a few minutes, he is back, followed by a friend of ours. It is an old friend who went back to visit his relatives in the old country. He had also done us the favor of taking some money to give to Aunt Dora. We help whenever we can. We had heard that our friend was already back, but had not seen him until now—he hadn't called or paid us a visit. Must have been busy.

Now he avoids my gaze. I feel uneasiness take hold of me when my husband asks me to sit down, his face betraying discomfort and sadness.

"Father is dead," he declares.

I know that he means my father since his own had passed away years ago.

"It is impossible," I say. "He promised me to live forever. It is impossible!"

I am absolutely sincere. And I start crying—from anger and frustration.

Mother had just passed away, and I felt guilty. I was not around—not because I did not want to be. Still, I felt distraught and scared. On the phone, I begged Dad: *"You are going to live forever!"*

He felt sorry for me, and he promised he would.

Now I screamed: *"You lied to me!* You promised me to live forever!"

And my sadness turned to anger. And this made it easier to bear the news.

There has been too much sorrow in my life.

I could not survive without the lies.

Do you understand? It sounds unreasonable and crazy. But have you been in a situation when everything seems beyond your control? When you feel betrayed by life itself? When you lose hope and begin to lie? When the distinction between "rational" and "irrational" becomes so blurred by brutal reality that even cease to matter?

You lie to yourself, to the people you love, and they, in turn, start to lie to you.

Life turns into one big lie.

Not even sacred relationships are exempted.

It is all just a matter of survival.

◆      ◆      ◆

The rain has stopped for a while—long enough for the moisture to evaporate from the wet surfaces and to turn the exposed slabs back into their natural light gray, almost white color. The sharp line between the wet and dry areas has vanished. I am slowly coming out of my reverie. The spell is over.

For a while, I had allowed myself to be duped by nature into believing in eternity. Now that I am back, I feel relaxed and at peace.

I hear a voice calling my name. It is Emmy, who lives in a cottage down the road. Today she is wearing her wooden sabot shoes, a colorful cotton dress, and a funny denim hat. She is holding a small bouquet of wild flowers in one hand and a wooden staff in the other.

"Hi," she chirps cheerfully, casting a glance at her sabots and flashing a smile.

"The road is muddy all the way. So much rain this summer . . ."

"What shall we do?" she inquires.

"Oh, I don't know," I say with a drawl.

"Well, how about going to the pub?" she suggests after some brief contemplation. "We can have some gin and tonic and sit outside and look at the panorama."

"Yeah, let's do that," I say, though I'm still not quite here.

We walk up the driveway and head toward the village pub.

# *Lost*

On a cold, wintry day, thousands of kilometers from the Monastery of St. Petka, the following Internet post appeared on my computer screen:

> *The Monastery of St. Petka lies in the folds of Mount Lyulin near Sofia . . . etc., etc . . . The compound includes a small church, housing, and economic facilities . . . etc., etc . . . The outer and inner wall abound in murals of saints and scenes from . . . etc., etc . . .*

To a monastery aficionado like me, it sounded intriguing, like a place I thought worth seeing—old and authentic. The economic facilities sounded good too, considering . . .

Well, most of that turned out to be a blatant advertisement; however, I am not complaining—just setting the scene for a memorable excursion.

Around ten o'clock in the morning of a hot August day, we set out on a short trip of approximately fifty kilometers to the Monastery of St. Petka. Already we felt that this was going to be an adventure since no one of the locals we had approached with the question "where is the Monastery of St. Petka located?" had been able to give us a straight answer. Indeed, they had shown plenty of good will, politely engaging us in long chats and conveying friendly smiles that, in fact, were nothing other than a pleasant way of avoiding telling us the simple truth: they had no idea.

As it turned out, the venerable saint was very popular in this region. There were so many churches and monasteries dedicated to her glory that it was hard to pinpoint a specific one. Eventually, we were able to conjure up a vague idea of the general area where this particular monastery was located. The estimated time to reach the destination was about two hours, taking into account the mountainous terrain, the uncertainty about the route, the anticipated congestion, and the poor road conditions. In fact, the trip took us close to four hours.

Not long after the start of our journey, there was a moment when we almost gave up and seriously contemplated the possibility of going back on foot. It was on account of a problem with the old car as strange noises had started coming from under its hood, which unnerved us. The interlude, though, was of a short duration—a few cans of oil poured into the motor seemed to take care of the problem. The noise was gone, and we were back on our way.

A few other unanticipated moments worth mentioning occurred: coming across a gigantic site of future highway, navigating through a number of villages we could not identify for lack of signs, and getting involved in more conversations with locals who kept ending their well-intentioned but endless explanations with "Anyway, at this crossing over there . . ." while pointing at the general direction one way and then the other ". . . there will be a sign and . . ."

The instructions invariably proved to be wrong.

Finally, we came to the curious conclusion that all the knowledgeable people—the ones who traveled these roads frequently—were not to be trusted on the matter of signs. After all, they had no need for them, and all they were doing was assuming notions not to be taken at face value. They simply would not believe us when we insisted there were no signs whatsoever—which added to our frustration. But I am digressing.

Our lucky break from the vicious cycle of trying to get on the right track came when I entered a small variety store in the town of Bankya and inquired of a salesgirl about directions. It was the customer paying for his groceries at the counter who volunteered the information, which for once was clear, short, and precise. A couple of blocks away, we learned that we have had again veered into the wrong direction. We were waved away from it by the driver of a yellow taxicab passing us. The smiling face that popped out of the driver's side window was none other than the guy with the groceries. So once again, we were straightened out by the same person—away from the wrong street—and cheerfully sent on our way. After that, we got lost only once more, but it was a short detour that did not contribute much to our delay.

The monastery stood at the top of a winding road that was covered in potholes, the asphalt eaten away at the edges by grass and water. In some places, it looked as though somebody had been trying to peel away the unseemly black ribbon that zigzagged across the green expanse. The monastery's compound appeared almost miraculously behind a curve, at the edge of a splendid meadow that bordered a pine forest. A building covered in bright murals met the eye, just as the Internet post had said. A door in front of the building opened into a passage that led to a court inside the compound. A small church and a couple of small houses came into view.

On the right side of the church itself white crosses marked the spots of a few tombs. It was peaceful, solemn, and beautiful. All was fresh, shiny, and very recent—as a matter of fact, still in construction.

A plaque told the story: once there had been an ancient church on this spot that had been destroyed ages ago. Now it was coming back to life—rebuilt. Well, but how do you bring to life the past? The new bright frescos covering the walls of a pretty, far-too-contemporary-looking building summoned memories of familiar movie sets. The two nuns who silently went about their duties looked genuine enough.

So we went into the church, walked along the narrow paths covered with flagstones, took a few photos, and left. A man working on the outside told us that the road we had come on continued farther on, to the left, and that it was nothing more than a dirt trail just a short distance past the monastery. Also, he informed us that it was a shortcut that led in the direction of our destination back home. We took it.

About half a mile away, we came upon a military station. We were told by a confidence-inspiring soldier that we were on the right path. In his estimation, this route would reduce our travelling time by at least fourfold! Without any hesitation we continued on.

Cautiously, we advanced along, thrown about the insides of the car with every bump and hollow of hardened mud we happened to hit upon or sink into. Eventually, we found ourselves surrounded by an endless green expanse under pale blue skies, covered in spots of dark green pine forests and rocky bare hills swept clean by winds from all vegetation except the prickly, hard, low grass. There was not a soul—not a bird, a rodent, or even an insect—about. Abandoned cottages falling into disrepair were scattered over the landscape, easily blending with the eternal solitude of the place. The sense of loneliness and isolation was overwhelming. It crept into our beings; it swallowed us.

I could hear the faint, persistent sound of incessant wailing—a medieval harmony of voices.

The bumpy, meandering road kept appearing and disappearing beyond hills and mounds until we reached the summit and found ourselves perched on its tip, staring at the blue horizon. We were sure that we had reached the end of the road and that there was nothing but a cavernous precipice beyond the point—an illusion that became obvious once we stepped outside the vehicle and saw deep furrows running along a steep-but-passable slope.

Euphoric with relief, we took the plunge. Ahead of us was the same green sea, just as vast, monotonous, and disorienting. *Time stood still.* Only the wailing kept drifting in waves passing us by in the far distance . . .

And then, all the enchantment and wonder was swept away by the sight, far below, of the blue, shimmering waters of a long and narrow dam and of the prosaic presence of a couple of silver cars parked by its shore. Not too far from there, the vague outlines of a village were visible. We were back to reality. The sound slowly died away, retreated.

The soldier was right. It had taken us no more than an hour to reach the small town of Breznik. There, we sat in the corner café, on fancy rattan chairs under an umbrella. We drank a cappuccino, ate crepe suzette with strawberry jam, and listened to the up-to-date, agreeable sound of American hip-hop, jazz, and rhythm. We took pictures of each other, and after lazily lingering for an hour, we jumped back into the car and headed to the coolness of our place in the hills of the next mountain.

The memory, only a couple of hours old, seemed strangely remote. All I remembered was the longing . . .